Kaplan Publishing are constantly finding new ways to make a difference to your studies and our exciting online resources really do offer something different to students looking for exam success.

This book comes with free MyKaplan online resources so that you can study anytime, anywhere. This **online resource is not sold separately** and is included in the price of the book.

Having purchased this book, you have access to the following online study materials:

CONTENT	Text	Kit
Electronic version of the book	✓	✓
Progress tests with instant answers	✓	
Mock assessments online	✓	✓
Material updates	✓	✓

How to access your online resources

Kaplan Financial students will already have a MyKaplan account and these extra resources will be available to you online. You do not need to register again, as this process was completed when you enrolled. If you are having problems accessing online materials, please ask your course administrator.

If you are not studying with Kaplan and did not purchase your book via a Kaplan website, to unlock your extra online resources please go to www.mykaplan.co.uk/addabook (even if you have set up an account and registered books previously). You will then need to enter the ISBN number (on the title page and back cover) and the unique pass key number contained in the scratch panel below to gain access. You will also be required to enter additional information during this process to set up or confirm your account details.

If you purchased through Kaplan Flexible Learning or via the Kaplan Publishing website you will automatically receive an e-mail invitation to MyKaplan. Please register your details using this email to gain access to your content. If you do not receive the e-mail or book content, please contact Kaplan Publishing.

Your Code and Information

This code can only be used once for the registration of one book online. This registration and your online content will expire when the final sittings for the examinations covered by this book have taken place. Please allow one hour from the time you submit your book details for us to process your request.

OXFORD AND CHERWELL VALLEY COLLEGE

065765

Please scratch the film to access your MyKaplan code.

Please be aware that this code is case-sensitive and you will need to include the dashes within the passcode, but not when entering the ISBN. For further technical support, please visit www.MyKaplan.co.uk

KAPLAN

PUBLISHING

AAT

AQ2016

Using Accounting Software

EXAM KIT
(for Sage 50 / Sage Instant)

This Exam Kit supports study for the following AAT qualifications:
AAT Foundation Certificate in Accounting – Level 2
AAT Foundation Diploma in Accounting and Business – Level 2
AAT Foundation Award in Accounting Software – Level 2
AAT Foundation Certificate in Accounting at SCQF Level 5

KAPLAN
PUBLISHING

British Library Cataloguing-in-Publication Data

A catalogue record for this book is available from the British Library.

Published by:

Kaplan Publishing UK

Unit 2 The Business Centre

Molly Millar's Lane

Wokingham

Berkshire

RG41 2QZ

ISBN: 978-0-85732-033-9

© Kaplan Financial Limited, 2017

Printed and bound in Great Britain.

CONTENTS

Features in this exam kit

In addition to providing a wide ranging bank of real exam style questions, we have also included in this kit:

- Paper specific information and advice on exam technique.

- Our recommended approach to make your revision for this particular subject as effective as possible.

You will find a wealth of other resources to help you with your studies on MyKaplan and AAT websites:

www.mykaplan.co.uk

www.aat.org.uk/

Quality and accuracy are of the upmost importance to us so if you spot an error in any of our products, please send an email to mykaplanreporting@kaplan.com with full details, or follow the link to the feedback form in MyKaplan.

Our Quality Co-ordinator will work with our technical team to verify the error and take action to ensure it is corrected in future editions

INDEX TO PRACTICE QUESTIONS

EXAM TECHNIQUE

- **Do not skip any of the material** in the syllabus.

- **Read each question** *very* carefully.

- **Double-check your answer** before committing yourself to it.

- Answer **every** question – if you do not know an answer to a multiple choice question or true/false question, you don't lose anything by guessing. Think carefully before you **guess**.

- If you are answering a multiple-choice question, **eliminate first those answers that you know are wrong**. Then choose the most appropriate answer from those that are left.

- **Don't panic** if you realise you've answered a question incorrectly. Getting one question wrong will not mean the difference between passing and failing

Computer-based exams – tips

- Do not attempt a CBA until you have **completed all study material** relating to it.

- On the AAT website there is a CBA demonstration. It is **ESSENTIAL** that you attempt this before your real CBA. You will become familiar with how to move around the CBA screens and the way that questions are formatted, increasing your confidence and speed in the actual exam.

- Be sure you understand how to use the **software** before you start the exam. If in doubt, ask the assessment centre staff to explain it to you.

- Questions are **displayed on the screen** and answers are entered using keyboard and mouse.

- In addition to the traditional multiple-choice question type, CBAs will also contain **other types of questions**, such as number entry questions, drag and drop, true/false, pick lists or drop down menus or hybrids of these.

- In some CBAs you will have to type in complete computations or written answers.

- You need to be sure you **know how to answer questions** of this type before you sit the exam, through practice.

PAPER SPECIFIC INFORMATION

THE EXAM

FORMAT OF THE ASSESSMENT

The assessment will consist of one part and will cover the following areas:-

Task	Title for topics within task range
1	Set up accounting software – Set up customer accounts
2	Set up accounting software – Set up supplier accounts
3	Set up accounting software – Enter information relating to the organisation at the beginning of an accounting period
4	Process sales and purchase transactions – Process sales invoices and credit notes
5	Process sales and purchase transactions – Process purchase invoices and credit notes
6	Process bank and cash transactions – Process receipts and payments for non-credit transactions
7	Process sales and purchase transactions – Allocate receipts from customers
8	Process sales and purchase transactions – Allocate payments to suppliers
9	Process bank and cash transactions – Process recurring receipts and payments
10	Process bank and cash transactions – Process petty cash receipts and payments
11	Perform period end routine tasks – Process journals
12	Perform period end routine tasks – Reconcile the bank statement
13	Produce reports – Produce routine reports for customers and suppliers, produce routine reports from the general ledger

- At the beginning of the assessment you will be required to set up the details of the company. This does not form part of the assessment standards therefore your tutor may assist you with this.

- At the end of the assessment you will be required to upload a number of reports from which your competency will be assessed. There is a checklist to help you make sure that you have all of the required documents, make sure you tick these off!

- Failure to upload the required documentation will result in no marks being allocated for the tasks to which they relate.

- Make sure that you read carefully what is required and ensure that your upload has been successful before submitting your assessment.

Learners will be assessed by a computer based assessment, and will be required to demonstrate competence (70%).

Time allowed

2 hours

 Always keep your eye on the clock and make sure you attempt all questions!

ACCOUNTING SOFTWARE

There are a number of different types of accounting software applicable to the AAT Using Accounting Software assessment. This Exam Kit uses **Sage 50 Accounts version 18.** This version of Sage is very similar to Sage Instant Accounts version 17 and therefore you should still be able to use this Exam Kit for Sage Instant, as well as many other accounting software packages, without too much difficulty, although you may find that some of the screen shots will differ.

Kaplan Publishing also produce a separate Study Text and Exam Kit for Sage One software, which is an online service and as such has functionality not covered in this book. Please check to ensure you have the correct study materials for your course and if using Sage One for your assessment, you are strongly advised to purchase the Using Accounting Software Exam Kit dedicated to Sage One.

KAPLAN'S RECOMMENDED REVISION APPROACH

QUESTION PRACTICE IS THE KEY TO SUCCESS

Success in professional examinations relies upon you acquiring a firm grasp of the required knowledge at the tuition phase. In order to be able to do the questions, knowledge is essential.

However, the difference between success and failure often hinges on your exam technique on the day and making the most of the revision phase of your studies.

The **Kaplan textbook** is the starting point, designed to provide the underpinning knowledge to tackle all questions. However, in the revision phase, poring over text books is not the answer.

The Kaplan workbook helps you consolidate your knowledge and understanding and is a useful tool to check whether you can remember key topic areas.

Kaplan pocket notes are designed to help you quickly revise a topic area, however you then need to practise questions. There is a need to progress to exam style questions as soon as possible, and to tie your exam technique and technical knowledge together.

The importance of question practice cannot be over-emphasised.

The recommended approach below is designed by expert tutors in the field, in conjunction with their knowledge of the examiner and the specimen assessment.

You need to practise as many questions as possible in the time you have left.

OUR AIM

Our aim is to get you to the stage where you can attempt exam questions confidently, to time, in a closed book environment, with no supplementary help (i.e. to simulate the real examination experience).

Practising your exam technique is also vitally important for you to assess your progress and identify areas of weakness that may need more attention in the final run up to the examination.

In order to achieve this we recognise that initially you may feel the need to practice some questions with open book help.

Good exam technique is vital.

THE KAPLAN UACS REVISION PLAN

Stage 1: Assess areas of strengths and weaknesses

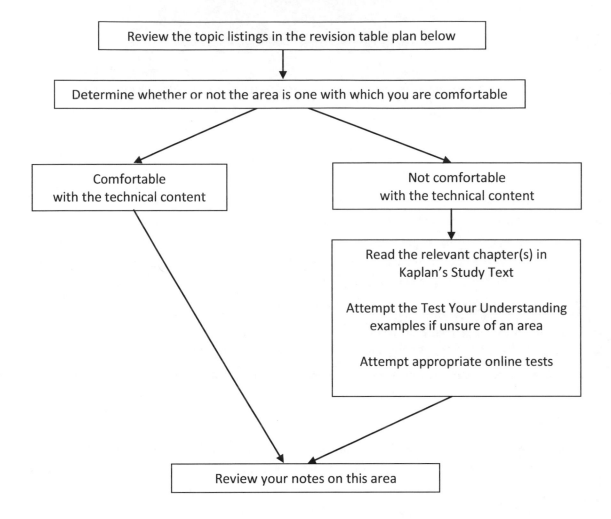

KAPLAN PUBLISHING

Stage 2: Practice questions

Follow the order of revision of topics as presented in this kit and attempt the questions in the order suggested.

Try to avoid referring to text books and notes and the model answer until you have completed your attempt.

Review your attempt with the model answer and assess how much of the answer you achieved.

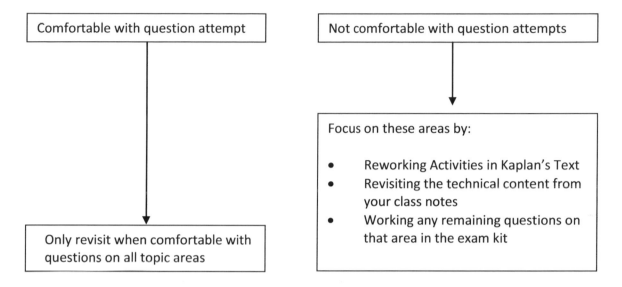

| Comfortable with question attempt | Not comfortable with question attempts |

Focus on these areas by:

- Reworking Activities in Kaplan's Text
- Revisiting the technical content from your class notes
- Working any remaining questions on that area in the exam kit

Only revisit when comfortable with questions on all topic areas

Stage 3: Final pre-exam revision

We recommend that you **attempt at least one two hour mock examination** containing a set of previously unseen exam standard questions.

Attempt the mock CBA online in timed, closed book conditions to simulate the real exam experience.

Section 1

PRACTICE QUESTIONS

PRACTICE PAPER 1

TOY SHOP

THE SITUATION

This assignment is based on an existing business, Toy Shop, a small manufacturer who has recently set up in business selling:

- Boxed Games
- Computer games
- Jigsaws

The owner of the business is James Free who operates as a sole trader.

At the start of the business James operated a manual bookkeeping system but has now decided that from 1st May 20XX the accounting system will become computerised.

You can assume that all documentation has been checked and authorised by James Free.

Some nominal ledger accounts have already been allocated suitable account codes. **You may need to amend or create other account codes.**

Set the company's Financial Year to start in April of the current year.

Their company details are:-
Toy Shop
64 Long Lane
Langhorne
North Yorkshire
YO21 3EJ

You are employed as an accounting technician.

The business is registered for VAT. The rate of VAT charged on all goods and services sold by Toy Shops is 20%.

Today's date is 31st May in the current financial year.

TASK 1

Refer to the customer listing below and set up customer records to open Sales Ledger accounts for each customer.

Customer account code	Customer name, address and contact details	Customer account details
BB01	Busy Bee Toys 832 High Street Oxford OX2 3WG	Credit limit: £4000 Payment Terms: 30 days Opening Balance: £349.20 (relates to invoice 021 dated 12th Apr)
FF02	Forming Fun 21 Newton Quay Knott Mill Manchester M6 3RJ	Credit limit: £4000 Payment Terms: 30 days Opening Balance: £99.60 (relates to invoice 035 dated 8th Apr)
SM03	Space Models 13 Central Street Perth Scotland SC4 8RQ	Credit limit: £3000 Payment Terms: 30 days Opening Balance: £1195.20 (relates to invoice 093 dated 10th Apr)
TP04	Teddy T's Party 3 Paradise Street Wokingham WO4 6QP	Credit limit: £7000 Payment Terms: 30 days Opening Balance: £579.60 (relates to invoice 1003 dated 17th Apr)

TASK 2

Refer to the supplier listing below and set up supplier records to open Purchase Ledger accounts for each supplier.

Supplier account code	Supplier name, address and contact details	Supplier account details
PL01	Abacus C & C Unit 31 Kitts Industrial Estate St Helens Lancs	Credit limit: £5500 Payment Terms: 30 days Opening Balance: £369.60 (relates to invoice B/1874 dated 2nd Apr)
PL02	Compugames Ltd 6 Jury Road Dublin Eire	Credit limit: £4000 Payment Terms: 30 days Opening Balance: £511.20 (relates to invoice 1087 dated 11th Apr)
PL03	Space Models 13 Central Street Perth Scotland SC4 8RQ	Credit limit: £2000 Payment Terms: 30 days Opening Balance: £306 (relates to invoice F-0193 dated 18th Apr)
PL04	Toys Unlimited 95 Cuscaden Road Edinburgh Scotland	Credit limit: £2000 Payment Terms: 30 days Opening Balance: £970.80 (relates to invoice W/032 dated 18th Apr)

TASK 3.1

Create new, or amend the following nominal codes

Account number	Account name
4000	Sales – Computer Games
4001	Sales – Boxed Games
4002	Sales – Jigsaws
5000	Purchases – Computer Games
5001	Purchases – Boxed Games
5002	Purchases – Jigsaws
3000	Capital
3260	Drawings
7100	Rent and Rates

TASK 3.2

Refer to the list of General ledger balances below. Enter the opening balances onto the computerised accounting system, making sure you select the appropriate general ledger account codes.

List of general ledger balances as at the **1st May**

Account name	DR	CR
	£	£
Furniture and fixtures	5800.00	
Motor Vehicles	3000.00	
Bank	4225.00	
Petty Cash	300.00	
Sales Ledger Control Account *	2223.60	
Purchase Ledger Control Account *		2157.60
Sales Tax control Account		543.00
Purchase Tax Control account	109.00	
Capital		20000.00
Drawings	355.00	
Sales – Computer Games		6080.00
Sales – Jigsaws		700.00
Sales – Boxed Games		1967.00
Purchases – Computer games	8000.00	
Purchases – Jigsaws	3200.00	
Purchases – Boxed Games	2465.00	
Office Stationery	53.00	
Electricity	167.00	
Rent and Rates	1550.00	
Note You do not need to enter these figures as you have already entered opening balances for customers and suppliers		

TASK 3.3

Transfer £500 from the bank current account to the bank deposit account. Enter this on the computerised accounting system using reference TRANS01 dated 1st May.

TASK 3.4

Print out the following reports and **identify and correct any errors**:

- Customer Address List
- Supplier Address List
- Period Trial Balance Report

TASK 4

Enter the following sales invoices and credit note onto the computerised accounting system.

	Toy Shops 64 Long Lane Langhorne North Yorkshire YO21 3EJ
Telephone: 0121 765 3213 Email: jp@toyshops.co.uk	
	Sales Invoice No 2021
	Date: 4th May 20XX

Busy Bee Toys
832 High Street
Oxford
OX2 3WG

Description	£
Computer Games	2585.00
VAT @ 20.00%	517.00
Total for payment	3102.00

Terms 30 days

Toy Shops
64 Long Lane
Langhorne
North Yorkshire
YO21 3EJ

Telephone: 0121 765 3213
Email: jp@toyshops.co.uk

Sales Invoice No 2022

Date: 4th May 20XX

Forming Fun
21 Newton Quay
Knott Mill
Manchester
M6 3RJ

Description	£
Boxed Games	500.00
VAT @ 20.00%	100.00
Total for payment	600.00

Terms 30 days

Toy Shops
64 Long Lane
Langhorne
North Yorkshire
YO21 3EJ

Telephone: 0121 765 3213
Email: jp@toyshops.co.uk

Sales Invoice No 2023

Date: 6th May 20XX

Teddy T's Party
3 Paradise Street
Wokingham
WO4 6QP

Description	£
Computer games	5000.00
VAT @ 20.00%	1000.00
Total for payment	6000.00

Terms 30 days

Toy Shops
64 Long Lane
Langhorne
North Yorkshire
YO21 3EJ

Telephone: 0121 765 3213
Email: jp@toyshops.co.uk

Credit Note No CN101

Date: 13th May 20XX

Teddy T's Party
3 Paradise Street
Wokingham
WO4 6QP

Description	£
Return faulty Computer games	320.00
VAT @ 20.00%	64.00
Total credit	384.00

TASK 5.1

Enter the following purchases invoices onto the computer system.

Date	A/C No.	Invoice Ref	Gross	Vat	Net	Computer games	Jigsaws	Boxed Games
3rd May	PL01	B/989	540.00	90.00	450.00	450.00		
5th May	PL02	145215	600.00	100.00	500.00			500.00
10th May	PL03	C-32632	1200.00	200.00	1000.00	1000.00		
10th May	PL04	12421	18.00	0.00	18.00		18.00	

TASK 5.2

Enter the following purchase credit note onto the computer system.

Date	Supplier	N/C	Credit Note Ref	Description	Details
15th May	Compugames	5000	11245	Computer Games	£88.00 Plus tax

TASK 6

Refer to the following cash sales and enter receipts into the computer. Use the bank current account for this transaction and enter 'cash sales' as the reference.

Date	Receipt Type	Gross	VAT	NET	Nominal code
13th May	Cash sale	1,200.00	200.00	1,000.00	4000
13th May	Cash sale	2,879.40	479.90	2,399.50	4001
20th May	Cash sale	995.00	0.00	995.00	4000

TASK 7

The following remittance advices were received from customers. Enter the receipts onto the computerised accounting system.

Busy Bee Toys
Remittance Advice
To: Toy Shop Date: 17 May 20XX   A cheque for £349.20 (number 100322) is attached in payment of invoice no 021.

Forming Fun
Remittance Advice
To: Toy Shop Date: 17 May 20XX   A cheque for £99.60 (number 267543) is attached in payment of invoice 035.

Teddy T's Party
BACS Remittance Advice
To: Toy Shop Date: 26 May 20XX   An amount of £195.60 has been paid directly into your bank account in payment of invoice 1003, including credit note CN101.

TASK 8

The following cheque payments were sent to suppliers; enter the payments on the accounts system. **Print off the relevant remittance advices**.

Date	Cheque No	Supplier	Amount	Details
22nd May	101333	Abacus C & C	369.60	Inv B/1874
22nd May	101334	Compugames	1005.60	Settle account in full.

TASK 9

On the 5th May you are asked to set up a monthly recurring payment for a Direct Debit. It is to pay Insurance for £100.00 (Exempt VAT) for a period of 12 months commencing on 31st May. There is no VAT on this transaction. The Insurance is payable to Galloway Union. Provide evidence by taking a screen shot and saving it as a 'Word' document. Ensure you process this month's transaction.

TASK 10

Enter the following petty cash payments onto the computerised accounting system.

Petty Cash Voucher			Petty Cash Voucher		
Date:		20.05.XX	**Date:**		21.05.XX
Voucher No:		012	**Voucher No:**		013
Details		£	**Details**		£
Subscriptions		32.00	Refreshments		10.40
(no Vat)			VAT		2.08
			Total		12.48
Main Ledger Code:		**8201**	**Main Ledger Code:**		**8205**
Authorised By;		*James Free*	**Authorised By;**		*James Free*
Receipt attached			Receipt attached		

TASK 11

Enter the following journal on the computerised accounting system.

Reference: JNL02			
Date	Account Name & Code	Dr	Cr
25th May	Drawings	2000.00	
	Bank		2000.00
Being the transfer of cash for James Free's personal use.			

TASK 12

(a)   Print out the following reports:

   (a)   Period Trial Balance Report

   (b)   Sales Day Book

   (c)   Sales Returns Day Book

   (d)   Purchase Day Book

   (e)   Customer Activity Report

   (f)   Supplier Activity Report

   (g)   Aged Creditors Report

   (h)   Aged Debtors Report

   (i)   Journal Day Book

TASK 13

Refer to the following email below from James Free.

E-Mail
From: James Free **To:** Accounts Technician **Date:** 19th May 20XX **Subject:**
Hello A credit customer Forming Fun has moved premises. Their new address is as follows: 100 Aventi Way St Albans Hertfordshire AL2 4PM Please ensure that this is updated on the computerised accounts system. Thanks James

Create a screen shot of the customer's record with the new address and save it as a 'Word' document.

TASK 14

The sum of £502.00 has been incorrectly been posted to the rent account instead of the gas account in error. Process the following journal to correct this using reference JNL03. Use today's date for the transaction.

<table>
<tr><td colspan="4" align="center">**Reference: JNL03**</td></tr>
<tr><td>**Date**</td><td>**Account Name & Code**</td><td>**Dr**</td><td>**Cr**</td></tr>
<tr><td>31st May</td><td>Gas</td><td>502.00</td><td></td></tr>
<tr><td></td><td>Rent & Rates</td><td></td><td>502.00</td></tr>
<tr><td colspan="4">Being the transfer of gas incorrectly posted to rent in error.</td></tr>
</table>

TASK 15

The following cheque payments were sent to suppliers; enter the payments on the accounts system and **produce the relevant remittance advices**.

Date	Supplier	Cheque No	Details	Amount
28th May	Space Models	101335	Payment of opening balance	306.00
28th May	Toys Unlimited	101336	Part payment invoice W/032	450.00
28th May	Abacus C & C	BACS	Payment of invoice B/989	540.00

TASK 16

The following payments were received from customers; enter the receipts on the accounts system, dated 29 May 20XX.

Customer	Cheque No	Details	Amount (£)
Busy Bee	104662	Invoice 2021	3102.00
Forming Fun	828100	Part payment invoice 2022	400.00
Teddy T's Party	672522	Payment of invoice 2023	6000.00

TASK 17

On 14th May a member of staff buys Computer Games paying you £264.00 in Cash. This is inclusive of 20% VAT. Enter this in the bank current account and use reference CSH41 for this transaction.

TASK 18

On 19th May, you sold a 'Jigsaw' to a customer and they paid £45.00 (Zero rated VAT) debit card. Enter this in the bank current account and use reference 'Debit Card' for this transaction.

TASK 19

A cheque you received from Forming Fun for £99.60 (Cheque No 267543) has been returned by the bank marked 'Refer to Drawer – Insufficient Funds'. Process this returned cheque through the records, dated 17th May.

TASK 20

You are asked to ensure that the petty cash account float is restored to a balance of £300.00 by bank transfer (dated 31st May). Enter this transaction onto the computerised system and use reference CSH25.

TASK 21

Toy Shop has been granted a bank loan for £10,000.00 and it has been received in to the bank current account on 31 May 20XX. Process the following journal to record this transaction (use ref JNL04).

Reference: JNL04			
Date	**Account Name & Code**	**Dr**	**Cr**
31st May	Bank Current Account	10000.00	
	Loan Account		10000.00
Being the proceeds received for a new loan.			

TASK 22

You are given the following bank statement and are asked to produce a bank reconciliation as at 31st May , processing any adjustments that may be necessary.

Friendly Bank plc

201 Main Road

Rochester

Kent

ME15 9JP

Toy Shops

64 Long Lane

Langthorne   31st May 20XX

North Yorkshire   Statement no: 0003

YO21 3EJ

Account number: 00678432

Statement of Account

Date: May 20XX	Details	Paid out £	Paid in £	Balance £
1 May	Opening balance			4225.00C
1 May	Transfer	500.00		3725.00C
13 May	Counter credit		1200.00	4925.00C
13 May	Counter credit		2879.40	7804.40C
14 May	Counter credit		264.00	8068.40C
17 May	Counter credit		349.20	8417.60C
17 May	Counter credit		99.60	8517.20C
19 May	Debit Card		45.00	8562.20C
20 May	Counter credit		995.00	9557.20C
22 May	Cheque 101333	369.60		9187.60C
23 May	Cheque 101334	1005.60		8182.00C
25 May	Counter debit Ref: JNL 02	2000.00		6182.00C
26 May	BACS: Teddy's T Party		195.60	6377.60C
28 May	Cheque 101336	450.00		5927.60C
29 May	Counter credit		3102.00	9029.60C
29 May	Counter credit		6000.00	15029.60C
29 May	Counter credit		400.00	15429.60C
30 May	BACS payment	540.00		14889.60C
31 May	Dishonoured cheque	99.60		14790.00C
31 May	Transfer	44.48		14745.52C
31 May	Direct Debit – Galloway Union	100.00		14645.52C
31 May	Bank charges	101.32		14544.20C
31 May	Loan		10000.00	24544.20C
	D = Debit C = Credit			

TASK 23

Print the following reports

(a)   Customer Activity (detailed) Report

(b)   Supplier Activity (detailed) Report

(c)   Period Trial Balance for the month of May

(d)   Audit Trail for May (detailed – transactions only)

(e)   Aged Debtors Analysis

(f)   Journal Day Book

(g)   Bank Reconciliation Report (showing reconciled transactions)

PRACTICE PAPER 2

CRAZY HAIR

THE SITUATION

This assignment is based on a new business, Crazy Hair, a small business recently set up selling hair products.

The owner of the business is Nina Birk who operates as a sole trader.

At the start of the business Nina operated a manual bookkeeping system but has now decided that from 1st May 20XX the accounting system will become computerised.

You can assume that all documentation has been checked and authorised by Nina Birk.

Some nominal ledger accounts have already been allocated suitable account codes. **You may need to amend or create other account codes.**

Crazy Hair's financial year starts in March of the current year.

Their company details are:-
Crazy Hair
34 Clapham Road
Clapham
London
SE3 2HR

You are employed as an accounting technician.

The business is registered for VAT. The rate of VAT charged on all goods and services sold by Crazy Hair is 20%.

Today's date is 31st May in the current financial year.

TASK 1

Refer to the customer listing below and set up customer records to open Sales Ledger accounts for each customer.

Customer account code	Customer name, address and contact details	Customer account details
104	Alfred Images Masuki Offices PO Box 5684 Birmingham B23 4RD	Credit limit: £8000 Payment Terms: 30 days Opening Balance: £1809.60 (relates to invoice 3352 dated 2nd April)
110	Figgaro Beta Studio 34 Knightsbridge Way Morden SE23 4KA	Credit limit: £6500 Payment Terms: 30 days Opening Balance: £3880.80 (relates to invoice 2856 dated 10th April)
118	Blades Alpha Studio 45 Key West London SE1 0JF	Credit limit: £6100 Payment Terms: 30 days Opening Balance: £2144.40 (relates to invoice 3345 dated 18th April)
122	Hair Studio Framlington Court Lee London SE4 7YH	Credit limit: £5000 Payment Terms: 30 days Opening Balance: £681.60 (relates to invoice 3098 dated 12th April)
138	Ribbons & Curls PO Box 1120 Canning Town London TN2 2EB	Credit limit: £5000 Payment Terms: 30 days Opening Balance: £391.20 (relates to invoice 3123 dated 12th April)

TASK 2

Refer to the supplier listing below and set up supplier records to open Purchase Ledger accounts for each supplier.

Supplier account code	Supplier name, address and contact details	Supplier account details
1134	Avada Cash & Carry 32 Surrey Quay Isle of Dogs E12 3NW	Credit limit: £5500 Payment Terms: 30 days Opening Balance: £4454.40 (relates to invoice C/251 dated 22nd April)
1138	Straightside Supplies Havering Place Holborn London WC1 2PP	Credit limit: £12000 Payment Terms: 30 days Opening Balance: £1839.60 (relates to invoice 9140 dated 11th April)
1165	Hair Supplies 43 St Helens Way London SE7 3RF	Credit limit: £4000 Payment Terms: 30 days Opening Balance: £818.40 (relates to invoice 0028 dated 11th April)
1185	Wig Specialists Retro Square 32 Wigmore Road London EC1V 3SG	Credit limit: £5000 Payment Terms: 30 days Opening Balance: £102.00 (relates to invoice S653 dated 18th April)

TASK 3.1

Create new, or amend the following nominal codes.

Account number	Account name	Account number	Account name
4000	Sales – Brushes	5000	Purchases – Brushes
4001	Sales – Combs	5001	Purchases – Combs
4002	Sales – Colours	5002	Purchases – Colours
4003	Sales – Hairdryers	5003	Purchases – Hairdryers
4004	Sales – Wigs	5004	Purchases – Wigs
4005	Cash Sales	3000	Capital
3260	Drawings		
7803	General Expenses		
7100	Rent and rates		

TASK 3.2

Refer to the list of General ledger balances below. Enter the opening balances into the computer, making sure you select the appropriate general ledger account codes.

List of general ledger balances as at the **1st May**

Account name	£	£
Motor Vehicle	24000.00	
Furniture and Fixtures	31000.00	
Bank	54210.81	
Petty Cash	200.00	
Sales Ledger Control Account *	8907.60	
Purchase Ledger Control Account*		7214.40
Sales Tax control Account		5550.00
Purchase Tax Control account	1507.94	
Capital		165000.00
Drawings	5000.00	
Sales – Brushes		345.00
Sales – Combs		187.00
Sales – Colours		3801.45
Sales – Hairdryers		758.00
Sales – Wigs		5600.00
Cash Sales		617.50
Purchases – Brushes	873.00	
Purchases – Combs	50.00	
Purchases – Colour	4200.00	
Purchases – Hairdryers	6310.00	
Purchases – Wigs	52814.00	
Note You do not need to enter these figures as you have already entered opening balances for customers and suppliers.		

TASK 3.3

(a) Print out the following reports and **identify and correct any errors**:

    (a) Customer Address List

    (b) Supplier Address List

    (c) Trial Balance

TASK 4

(a)   Enter the following sales invoices onto the computer.

Crazy Hair

Crazy Hair
34 Clapham Road
Clapham
London
SE3 2HR

Account No: 138
Invoice No: 3353

Date: 12 May 20XX

Ribbons & Curls
PO Box 1120
Canning Town
London
TN2 2EB

Quantity	Description	Unit Price	Net Cost	Tax	Gross	Nominal code
10	Colours	14.10	141.00	28.20	169.20	4002

Terms 30 days

Crazy Hair
34 Clapham Road
Clapham
London
SE3 2HR

Account No: 104
Invoice No: 3354

Date: 12 May 20XX

Alfred Images
Masuki Offices
PO Box 5684
Birmingham
B23 4RD

Quantity	Description	Unit Price	Net Cost	Tax	Gross	Nominal code
50	Brushes	11.62	581.00	116.20	697.20	4000

Terms 30 days

Crazy Hair
34 Clapham Road
Clapham
London
SE3 2HR

Account No: 110
Invoice No: 3355

Date: 13th May 20XX

Figgaro
Beta Studio
34 Knightsbridge Way
Morden
SE23 4KA

Quantity	Description	Unit Price	Net Cost	Tax	Gross	Nominal code
12	Hairdryers	55.00	660.00	132.00	792.00	4003

Terms 30 days

Crazy Hair
34 Clapham Road
Clapham
London
SE3 2HR

Account No: 118
Invoice No: 3356

Date: 15th May 20XX

Blades
Alpha Studio
45 Key West
London
SE1 0JF

Quantity	Description	Unit Price	Net Cost	Tax	Gross	Nominal code
8	Wigs	210.72	1685.76	337.15	2022.91	4004
3	Hairdryers	67.80	203.40	40.68	244.08	4003

Terms 30 days

Crazy Hair
34 Clapham Road
Clapham
London
SE3 2HR

Account No: 122
Invoice No: 3357

Date: 18 May 20XX

Hair Studio
Framlington Court
Lee
London
SE4 7YH

Quantity	Description	Unit Price	Net Cost	Tax	Gross	Nominal code
12	Brushes	26.40	316.80	63.36	380.16	4000
4	Wigs	220.48	881.92	176.38	1058.30	4004
16	Colours	14.40	230.40	46.08	276.48	4002

Terms 30 days

(b) On 25th May you send a credit note (CN23) to Alfred Images (Account No 104) for brushes. The total is £67.20 which includes tax.

TASK 5

(a) Enter the purchases invoices into the computer.

Date	A/C No.	Invoice Ref	Description	Nominal Code	Net	Vat	Gross
11 May	1138	3362	Brushes	5000	191.60	38.32	229.92
11 May	1134	C/910	Colours	5002	954.00	190.80	1144.80
13 May	1165	0814	Hairdryers	5003	178.56	0.00	178.56
14 May	1185	S1198	Wigs	5004	3393.60	678.72	4072.32

(b) Enter the following purchase credit note onto the computer system.

Date	A/C No	Supplier	N/C	Credit Note Ref	Amount
18 May	1185	Wigs Specialist	5004	C3223	123.24 Including Vat

TASK 6

Enter the following petty cash payments into the computer:

Date	Ref	Nominal Code	Net	VAT	Gross
19 May	CSH 86	7400	33.60	6.72	40.32
20 May	CSH 87	7501	4.51	0.00	4.51

TASK 7

The following payments were received from customers; enter the receipts on the accounts system.

Date	Receipt type	Customer	Amount	Details
20 May	Cheque No: 183001	Alfred Images	1809.60	Payment for invoice 3352
21 May	Cheque No: 654255	Blades	2144.40	Payment for invoice 3345
21 May	BACS	Figgaro	3880.80	Payment for invoice 2856
21 May	Cheque No: 452221	Hair Studio	681.60	Payment for invoice 3098

TASK 8

The following cheque payments were sent to suppliers; enter the payments on the accounts system dated 31st May and **produce the relevant remittance advices**.

Supplier	Cheque No:	Amount	Details
Wigs Specialist	163455	£102.00	Payment for invoice S653
Avada Cash & Carry	163456	£4454.40	Payment for invoice C/251
Hair Supplies	163457	£818.40	Payment for invoice 0028

TASK 9

On the 31st May, you are asked to set up a monthly standing order for rent for £500 (exempt VAT) for a period of 12 months commencing 31st May. Rent is payable to KH & Sons.

(a)   Take a screen shot of setting up the recurring entry for Rent

(b)   Process the first payment

TASK 10

On the 20th May, a member of staff purchases a 'Brush' from you and pays Crazy Hair a total of £21.00 in cash. This is inclusive of VAT of £3.50. Enter this in the bank current account and use reference 1001 for this transaction.

TASK 11

Enter the following journal

Ref : JH12			
Date	Account Name & Code	Dr	Cr
24 May	Drawings	440.00	
	Bank		440.00
Being the transfer of cash for personal use.			

TASK 12

(a) Refer to the following email below from Frances Williams

E-Mail
From: Frances Williams
Date: 19th May 20XX
Subject: Customer change of address
Hello
A credit customer Ribbons and Curls has moved premises. New address as follows: 122 Devonshire Road Cranbrook London SE1 2AB Please ensure that this is updated on the computerised accounts system.
Thanks Frances

(b) Create a screen shot of the customer's record showing the change of address and save it as a 'Word' document. Use a suitable file name to save the document.

TASK 13

A cheque you received from Hair Studio for £681.60 (Cheque No 452221) has been returned by the bank marked 'Refer to Drawer – Insufficient Funds'. Process this returned cheque through the records, dated 21st May.

TASK 14

On 31st May you transfer £30.52 from the Bank account to the petty cash account. Use reference TRF01.

TASK 15

You are given the following bank statement and are asked to produce a bank reconciliation at 31st May, processing any adjustments that may be necessary. Ensure that the direct debit for Coopers Union is coded to Premises Insurance costs. There is no VAT applicable on both direct debits.

Nice Bank plc
201 Main Road
Rochester
Kent
ME15 9JP

Crazy Hair
34 Clapham Road
London
SE3 2HR

31st May 20XX
Statement no: 0012

Account number: 32543211

Statement of Account

Date: May 20XX	Details	Paid out £	Paid in £	Balance £
01 May	Opening balance			54210.81C
14 May	Counter credit		1809.60	56020.41C
20 May	Counter credit		2144.40	58164.81C
20 May	BACS		3880.80	62045.61C
20 May	Counter credit		681.60	62727.21C
20 May	Counter credit		21.00	62748.21C
24 May	Dishonoured cheque	681.60		62066.61C
24 May	Counter Debit	440.00		61626.61C
24 May	Direct Debit – Coopers Union	168.00		61458.61C
24 May	Counter Debit	30.52		61428.09C
31 May	Direct Debit – Electricity	66.94		61361.15C
31 May	Bank Charges	27.11		61334.04C
31 May	KH & Sons	500.00		60834.04C
	D = Debit C = Credit			

TASK 16

Print the following reports

(a)   Customer Address List

(b)   Sales Day Book

(c)   Sales Returns Day Book

(d)   Purchases Day Book

(e)   Customer Activity (detailed report)

(f)   Supplier Activity (detailed report)

(g)   Period Trial Balance for the month of May

(h)   Audit Trail for May only (summary)

(i)   Aged Creditors (summary)

(j)   Aged Debtors (summary)

(k)   Nominal Ledger Activity Report for the following:

     1.1.1.   Bank Current Account

     1.1.2.   Petty Cash Account

(l)   Bank Reconciliation Report (reconciled transactions)

PRACTICE PAPER 3

SHOES 4U

THE SITUATION

This assignment is based on an existing organisation, Shoes 4U, a small business selling ladies and men's shoes.

The owner of the business is Dennis Cope who operates as a sole trader.

At the start of the business Dennis operated a manual bookkeeping system but has now decided that from 1st June 20XX the accounting system will become computerised.

You can assume that all documentation has been checked by Dennis Cope.

Some nominal ledger accounts have already been allocated suitable account codes. **You may need to amend or create other account codes.**

Shoes 4U's financial year starts in January of the current year.

Their company details are:-

Shoes 4U

85 Barrington Close

Carlisle

Cumbria

C41 3ED

You are employed as an accounting technician.

The business is registered for VAT. The rate of VAT charged on all goods and services sold by Shoes 4U is 20%.

Today's date is 30th June in the current financial year.

TASK 1

Refer to the customer listing below and set up customer records to open Sales Ledger accounts for each customer.

Customer account code	Customer name, address and contact details	Customer account details
SL186	Beckers Gate Ltd Butchergate Carlisle Cumbria C41 1SG	Credit limit: £5000 Payment Terms: 30 days Opening Balance: £4811.88 (relates to invoice 1613 dated 22nd May)
SL213	Eaton Bowls Club Seaton Street St Neots Cambs PE19 8EF	Credit limit: £3000 Payment Terms: 30 days Opening Balance: £961.98 (relates to invoice 1582 dated 10th May)
SL302	Jones Footwear Scotby Village Carlisle Cumbria C44 8BP	Credit limit: £6000 Payment Terms: 30 days Opening Balance: £3828.75 (relates to invoice 1596 dated 28th May)
SL307	Dickens Ladies Footwear 17 Royal Square Bleachfield North Yorkshire YO87 9AD	Credit limit: £11000 Payment Terms: 30 days Opening Balance: £783.66 (relates to invoice 1601 dated 21st May)

TASK 2

Refer to the supplier listing below and set up supplier records to open Purchase Ledger accounts for each supplier.

Supplier account code	Supplier name, address and contact details	Supplier account details
PL112	Bootsy & Smudge Ltd Factory Road Stilton Cambs PE7 3RP	Credit limit: £4000 Payment Terms: 30 days Opening Balance: £2881.26 (relates to invoice B/468 dated 22nd May)
PL168	Briggsthorpe Boots Long Buckby Wharf Long Buckby Northampton NN4 9UW	Credit limit: £50000 Payment Terms: 30 days Opening Balance: £43200.00 (relates to invoice 0001087 dated 18th May)
PL172	Gallows Fashion 18 The Crescent Pickford Cambs PE7 8QV	Credit limit: £2000 Payment Terms: 30 days Opening Balance: £400.00 (relates to invoice G-01239 dated 16th May)
PL173	Dickens Ladies Footwear 17 Royal Square Bleachfield North Yorkshire YO87 9AD	Credit limit: £2000 Payment Terms: 30 days Opening Balance: £567.00 (relates to invoice 06345 dated 16th May)

TASK 3.1

Create or amend the following nominal codes:

Account number	Account name
4000	Sales – Men's Footwear
4001	Sales – Ladies Footwear
4002	Cash Sales
5000	Purchases – Men's Footwear
5001	Purchases – Ladies Footwear
3000	Capital
3260	Drawings

TASK 3.2

Refer to the list of General ledger balances below. Enter the opening balances into the computer, making sure you select the appropriate general ledger account codes.

List of general ledger balances as at the 1st June

Account name	£	£
Freehold Property	72000.00	
Motor Vehicles	7500.00	
Furniture and Fixtures	9000.00	
Bank	19363.00	
Petty Cash	200.00	
Sales Ledger Control *	10386.27	
Purchase Ledger Control *		47048.26
Sales Tax control Account		3402.35
Purchase Tax Control account	1130.00	
Capital		30000.00
Drawings	600.00	
Sales – Men's Footwear		79320.00
Sales – Ladies Footwear		43210.00
Cash Sales		6798.00
Purchases – Men's Footwear	55432.00	
Purchases – Ladies Footwear	23410.00	
Advertising	7231.00	
Telephone	866.00	
Rent	1263.00	
Electricity	567.34	
Office Stationery	830.00	
Note You do not need to enter these figures as you have already entered opening balances for customers and suppliers		

TASK 3.3

Transfer £5000 from the bank current account to the bank deposit account, dated 1st June. Use TRF01 as the reference.

TASK 3.4

(1)   Print out the following reports and identify and correct any errors:

(a)   Customer Address list

(b)   Supplier Address List

(c)   Period Trial Balance Report

TASK 4

Enter the following sales invoices and credit notes on to the computer.

Shoes 4u
85 Barrington Close
Carlisle
Cumbria
C41 3ED

Sales Invoice No: 1622
Date: 4th June 20XX

Becker Gate Ltd
Butchergate
Carlisle
Cumbria
C41 1SG

Description	£
Men's Footwear	450.00
VAT @ 20.00%	90.00
Total for payment	540.00

Terms 30 days

Shoes 4u
85 Barrington Close
Carlisle
Cumbria
C41 3ED

Sales Invoice No: 1623
Date: 6th June 20XX

Eaton Bowls Club
Seaton Street
St Neots
Cambs
PE19 8EF

Description	£
Men's Footwear	1385.00
VAT @ 20.00%	277.00
Total for payment	1662.00

Terms 30 days

Shoes 4u
85 Barrington Close
Carlisle
Cumbria
C41 3ED

Sales Invoice No: 1624
Date: 14th June 20XX

Dickens Ladies Footwear
17 Royal Square
Bleachfield
North Yorkshire
YO87 9AD

Description	£
Men's Footwear	450.00
Ladies Footwear	1850.00
VAT @ 20.00%	460.00
Total for payment	2760.00

Terms 30 days

Shoes 4u
85 Barrington Close
Carlisle
Cumbria
C41 3ED

Sales Invoice No: 1625
Date: 17th June 20XX

Jones Footwear
Scotby Village
Carlisle
Cumbria
C44 8BP

Description	£
Ladies Footwear	1175.75
VAT @ 20.00%	235.15
Total for payment	1410.90

Terms 30 days

Shoes 4u
85 Barrington Close
Carlisle
Cumbria
C41 3ED

Credit Note No: CR10
Date: 8th June 20XX

Dickens Ladies Footwear
17 Royal Square
Bleachfield
North Yorkshire
YO87 9AD

Description	£
Returned Ladies Footwear – Damage in transit	235.00
VAT @ 20.00%	47.00
Total for payment	282.00

Terms 30 days

TASK 5

Enter supplier invoices into the computer.

Date	Description	N/C	Invoice Ref	Net	Vat	Gross
2 June	Bootsy & Smudge Ltd	5001	B/752	300.00	60.00	360.00
10 June	Briggsthorpe Boots	5000	12350	2500.00	500.00	3000.00
12 June	Gallows Fashion	5000	G-2285	2500.00	500.00	3000.00
13 June	Bootsy & Smudge Ltd	5001	B/753	200.00	40.00	240.00

TASK 6

On the 23rd June, a member of staff purchases 'Mens Footwear' from you and pays you a total of £77.59 in cash. This is inclusive of VAT. Enter this in to the bank current account and use reference F027 for the transaction.

TASK 7

The following payments were received from customers; enter the receipts on the accounts system.

Date	A/c No	Customer	Cheque No	Details	Amount £
11 June	SL186	Beckers Gate Ltd	199846	Payment for invoice 1613	4811.88
14 June	SL213	Eaton Bowls Club	107654	Payment for invoice 1582	961.98
14 June	SL302	Jones Footwear	244536	Payment for invoice 1596	3828.75

TASK 8

The following cheque payments were sent to suppliers; enter the payments on the accounts system and **raise the relevant remittance advices**.

Date	A/c No	Supplier	Cheque No	Details	Amount £
18 June	PL172	Gallows Fashion	109887	Payment for invoice G-01239	400.00
18 June	PL168	Briggsthorpe Boots	109888	Part Payment for invoice 0001087	23300.00

TASK 9.1

Refer to the following standing order schedule:

- Set up a recurring entry as shown in the standing order schedule below.
- Print a screen shot of the screen setting up the recurring entry.
- Process the first payment.

Details	Amount	Frequency of payment	Total number of payments	Payment start date 20XX	Payment finish date 20XX
Electricity (ECBE Ltd)	£193.00 No Vat	Quarterly	4	25th June 20XX	25th March 20XX

TASK 9.2

Refer to the following BACS receipt schedule:

- Set up a recurring entry as shown in the schedule below.
- Print a screen shot of the screen setting up the recurring entry.
- Process the first receipt.

Details	Amount	Frequency of receipt	Total number of receipts	Start date 20XX	Finish date 20XX
Rent	£1500 (no VAT)	Quarterly	4	30th June 20XX	30th March 20XX

TASK 10.1

The following items were paid by cash

Petty Cash Voucher		
Date:	05.06.XX	
Voucher No:	010	
Details		£
Refreshments		9.90
(no Vat)		
Main Ledger Code:	8205	
Authorised By;	Dennis Cope	
Receipt attached		

Petty Cash Voucher		
Date:	10.06.XX	
Voucher No:	011	
Details		£
Office stationery		11.25
VAT		2.25
Total		13.50
Main Ledger Code:	7504	
Authorised By;	Dennis Cope	
Receipt attached		

TASK 10.2

Reimburse the petty cash tin with £23.40 which has been withdrawn from the bank. Use 10th June 20XX and reference TRF02 for this transaction.

TASK 11

Enter the following journal.

JOURNAL No: 209			
Date	Account Name & Code	Dr	Cr
25th June	Drawings	3200.00	
	Bank		3200.00

Being the transfer of cash for personal use.

TASK 12

On 22nd June you sold Ladies Footwear to a customer and they paid £54.00 debit card inclusive of tax £9.00. Use reference DC03.

TASK 13

A cheque you received from Eaton Bowls Club for £961.98 (Cheque no: 107654) has been returned by the bank marked 'Refer to Drawer – Insufficient Funds'. Process this returned cheque through the records, dated 14th June.

TASK 14

Refer to the following email below from Dennis Cope.

E-Mail
From: Dennis Cope
To: Accounts Technician
Date: 30th June 20XX
Subject: Customer write off

Hello

In view of Eaton Bowls Club and cheque that was returned by their bankers, I have decided that we should write off the balance of their account at 30th June 20XX. Please ensure that this is done.

Thanks

Dennis Cope

TASK 15

You are given the following bank statement and are asked to produce a bank reconciliation at 30th June 20XX, processing any adjustments that may be necessary. The BACS receipt on the 25th June relates to Rent Received.

Friendly Bank plc

201 Lake Rise
Whitewater
Cumbria
C21 9JF

STATEMENT : ACCOUNT No 22567767

Shoes 4U   30th June 20XX
85 Barrington Close   Statement 0011
Carlisle
Cumbria
C41 3ED

Date June 20XX	Detail	Paid out £	Paid in £	Balance
1st June	Opening Balance			19363.00C
1st June	Transfer	5000.00		14363.00C
14th June	Counter debit	23.40		14339.60C
14th June	Cheque receipt		4811.88	19151.48C
14th June	Cheque receipt		961.98	20113.46C
16th June	Dishonoured Cheque	961.98		19151.48C
18th June	Cheque 109888	23300.00		4148.52D
21st June	Debit Card transaction		54.00	4094.52D
22nd June	DD – ECBE Ltd	193.00		4287.52D
23rd June	Counter credit		77.59	4209.93D
25th June	Counter Debit	3200.00		7409.93D
25th June	Bank Charges	50.00		7459.93D
30th June	Counter Credit		3828.75	3631.18D
30th June	BACS receipt		1500.00	2131.18D

| C = Credit | D = Debit | DD – Direct Debit |

TASK 16

(a)   Print out the following reports:

    (1)   Period Trial Balance Report

    (2)   Sales Day Book

    (3)   Customer Activity Report

    (4)   Supplier Activity Report

    (5)   Aged Creditors Report (detailed)

    (6)   Aged Debtors Report (detailed)

    (7)   Nominal Ledger Activity Report for the following accounts

        (a)   Bank Current Account

        (b)   Petty Cash Account

    (8)   Audit trail

    (9)   Bank Reconciliation (Reconciled transactions)

PRACTICE PAPER 4

SPORTS GEAR

THE SITUATION

This assignment is based on an existing business, **Sports Gear**, who has recently set up in business selling sports equipment.

The owner of the business is Nina Birk who operates as a sole trader.

At the start of the business Nina operated a manual bookkeeping system but has now decided that from 1st July 20XX the accounting system will become computerised.

You can assume that all documentation has been checked and authorised by Nina Birk.

Some nominal ledger accounts have already been allocated suitable account codes. **You may need to amend or create other account codes.**

Sport Gear's Financial Year starts in January.

Their company details are:-

Sports Gear

34 Hockey Avenue

Tennison

London

EC1V 1NY

You are employed as an accounting technician.

The business is registered for VAT. The rate of VAT charged on all goods and services sold by Sports Gear is 20%.

Today's date is 31st July in the current financial year.

TASK 1

Refer to the customer listing below and set up customer records to open Sales Ledger accounts for each customer.

Customer account code	Customer name, address and contact details	Customer account details
SL01	J Hollingham 56 Glencoe Avenue Gants Hill Ilford Essex IG1 6FR	Credit limit: £5000 Payment Terms: 30 days Opening Balance: £3462.12 (relates to invoice 1001 dated 12th June 20XX)
SL02	Paul McCallum 34 St Albans Road Seven Kings Essex IG7 8DS	Credit limit: £9500 Payment Terms: 30 days Opening Balance: £514.68 (relates to invoice 0087 dated 10th June 20XX)
SL03	Kerry Jenkins 34 Gloucester Road Gillingham Kent ME14 3TL	Credit limit: £8000 Payment Terms: 30 days Opening Balance: £758.34 (relates to invoice 0093 dated 8th June 20XX)
SL04	Harry Bucket 54 Dale Road Harrogate North Yorks Y02 3HN	Credit limit: £12000 Payment Terms: 30 days Opening Balance: £2767.34 (relates to invoice 1003 dated 12th June 20XX)
SL05	Evelyn Rose 98 Crabtree Drive Bromley Kent DA3 6AY	Credit limit: £7000 Payment Terms: 30 days Opening Balance: £942.98 (relates to invoice 1004 dated 12th June 20XX)

TASK 2

Refer to the supplier listing below and set up supplier records to open Purchase Ledger account for each supplier.

Supplier account code	Supplier name, address and contact details	Supplier account details
PL01	Radcliff and Sons Orient House Lower Clapham London E1 2RH	Credit limit: £15500 Payment Terms: 30 days Opening Balance: £5362.14 (relates to invoice 1874 dated 22nd June 20XX)
PL02	Tennison Bros White Cottage London WC1 6YD	Credit limit: £11000 Payment Terms: 30 days Opening Balance: £2801.00 (relates to invoice B-321 dated 11th June 20XX)
PL03	Skipton & Co 22 Chatsworth Lane Water Square London EC1V 6NJ	Credit limit: £9000 Payment Terms: 30 days Opening Balance: £501.00 (relates to invoice 1087 dated 11th June 20XX)
PL04	Evelyn Rose 98 Crabtree Drive Bromley Kent DA3 6AY	Credit limit: £3000 Payment Terms: 30 days Opening Balance: £250.00 (relates to invoice A193 dated 18th June 20XX)

TASK 3.1

Create or amend the following nominal codes.

Account number	Account name
4000	Sales – Tennis Racquets
4001	Sales – Exercise Bikes
4002	Sales – Golf Clubs
4003	Sales – Fishing Rods
5000	Purchases – Tennis Racquets
5001	Purchases – Exercise Bikes
5002	Purchases – Golf Clubs
5003	Purchases – Fishing Rods
3000	Capital
3260	Drawings
7803	Postage

TASK 3.2

Refer to the list of General ledger balances below. Enter the opening balances into the computer, making sure you select the appropriate general ledger account codes.

List of general ledger balances as at 01.07.20XX

Account name	£	£
Motor Vehicle	15500.00	
Furniture and Fixtures	18000.00	
Office Equipment	8430.00	
Bank	3325.40	
Petty Cash	300.00	
Sales Ledger Control Account*	8445.46	
Purchase Ledger Control Account*		8914.14
Sales Tax control Account		3458.00
Purchase Tax Control account	1120.00	
Capital		52000.00
Drawings	1294.00	
Sales – Tennis Racquets		13266.78
Sales – Exercise Bikes		22310.00
Sales – Golf Clubs		9543.00
Sales – Fishing Rods		5644.00
Purchases – Tennis Racquets	21354.00	
Purchases – Exercise Bikes	25610.00	
Purchases – Golf Clubs	5475.00	
Purchases – Fishing Rods	4796.00	
Office Stationery	430.00	
Postage	560.00	
Electricity	496.06	
Note You do not need to enter these figures as you have already entered opening balances for customers and suppliers		

TASK 3.3

(a)   Print out the following reports and **identify and correct any errors:**

Customer Address list

Supplier Address List

Period Trial Balance Report

TASK 4

Enter the following sales invoices and credit notes onto the computer.

INVOICE

Sports Gear

34 Hockey Avenue

Tennison

London

EC1V 1NY

Account No: SL01   Date: 4 July 20XX

Invoice No: 1052

J Hollingham

56 Glencoe Avenue

Gants Hill

Ilford

Essex

IG1 6FR

Quantity	Description	Unit Price	Net £	Tax £	Gross £	Nominal code
20	Tennis Racquets	44.10	882.00	176.40	1058.40	4000
10	Exercise Bikes	102.36	1023.60	204.72	1228.32	4001
6	Fishing Rods	54.00	324.00	64.80	388.80	4003

Terms 30 days

INVOICE

Sports Gear

34 Hockey Avenue

Tennison

London

EC1V 1NY

Account No: SL03   Date: 6 July 20XX

Invoice No: 1053

Kerry Jenkins

Gloucester Road

Gillingham

Kent

ME14 3TL

Quantity	Description	Unit Price	Net £	Tax £	Gross £	Nominal code
3	Tennis Racquets	44.10	132.30	26.46	158.76	4000

Terms 30 days

INVOICE
Sports Gear
34 Hockey Avenue
Tennison
London
EC1V 1NY

Account No: SL04   Date: 8 July 20XX
Invoice No: 1054

Harry Bucket
54 Dale Road
Yorkshire
YO2 3HN

Quantity	Description	Unit Price	Net £	Tax £	Gross £	Nominal code
18	Golf Clubs	84.10	1513.80	302.76	1816.56	4002

Terms 30 days

CREDIT NOTE
Sports Gear
34 Hockey Avenue
Tennison
London
EC1V 1NY

Account No: SL01   Date: 17 July 20XX
Invoice No: CR34

J Hollingham
56 Glencoe Avenue
Gants Hill
Ilford
Essex
IG1 6FR

Description	£
Return faulty Exercise Bike	510.63
VAT @ 20.0%	102.12
Total credit	612.75

TASK 5

(a)   Enter the purchases invoices into the computer.

Date	A/C No.	Invoice Ref	Description	Net	Vat	Gross	Nominal code
3 July	PL01	1099	Tennis Racquets	550.00	110.00	660.00	5000
5 July	PL02	B – 1147	Exercise Bikes	320.00	64.00	384.00	5001
5 July	PL02	B – 1147	Postage	35.00	0.00	35.00	7803
10 July	PL03	2785	Golf Clubs	938.00	187.60	1125.60	5002
10 July	PL04	A/5698	Fishing Rods	671.00	134.20	805.20	5003

(b)   On 19th July, you receive a credit note (CX432) from Skipton & Co (Account No PL03) for two Golf Clubs that had been returned to them. The total credit note is for 109.45 plus sales tax of 20%.

TASK 6

Refer to the following cash sales and enter receipts into the bank current account on the computer.

Date	Receipt ref	Gross	VAT	NET	Nominal code
13 July	REC101	1,200.00	200.00	1,000.00	4000
15 July	REC102	2,879.40	479.90	2,399.50	4001
15 July	REC103	1,194.90	199.15	995.75	4000

TASK 7

The following payments were received from customers; enter the receipts on the accounts system.

Date	Receipt type	Customer	Amount	Details
19 July	Cheque No. 542321	J Hollingham	2849.37	Payment for invoice 1001 including credit note CR34
12 July	Cheque No. 222547	Kerry Jenkins	758.34	Payment for invoice 0093
13 July	BACS	Harry Bucket	2767.34	Payment for invoice 1003

TASK 8

The following cheque payments were sent to suppliers; enter the payments on the accounts system and **raise the relevant remittance advices.**

Date	Cheque No:	Supplier	Amount	Details
14th July	170012	Radcliff & Sons	5362.14	Payment for invoice 1874
17th July	170013	Tennison Bros	2801.00	Payment for invoice B-321

TASK 9

You are asked to set up a monthly standing order for Insurance for £100.00 (Exempt VAT) for a period of 12 months commencing on 28th July. There is no VAT on this transaction. The Insurance is payable to Ipswich Union. Take a screenshot of the details and save as a 'Word' document with a suitable file name. Process July's payment.

TASK 10

Enter the Petty cash payments into the computer

Petty Cash Voucher	
Date:	10.07.XX
Voucher No:	152
Details	£
Stationery (no Vat)	19.90
Main Ledger Code:	7504
Authorised By;	*Nina Birk*
Receipt attached	

Petty Cash Voucher	
Date:	20.07.XX
Voucher No:	187
Details	£
Postage	343.55
VAT	68.71
Total	412.26
Main Ledger Code:	7803
Authorised By;	*Nina Birk*
Receipt attached	

TASK 11

Enter the following journal

Ref : JNL004			
Date	Account Name & Code	Dr	Cr
25.07.XX	Drawings	3,441.00	
	Bank		3,441.00
Being the transfer of cash for personal use.			

TASK 12

Refer to the following email below from Nina Birk and save a screenshot of your work and save with a suitable file name.

E-Mail
From: Nina Birk
Date: 19th July 20XX
Subject: Customer change of address

Hello

A credit customer Harry Bucket has moved premises. New address as follows:

137 Chester Road

Capel Corner

CR3 2SA

Telephone: 08459 754 256

Please ensure that this is updated on the computerised accounts system.

Thanks

Nina

TASK 13

The following cheque payments were sent to suppliers; enter the payments on the accounts system.

Date	A/c No	Supplier	Cheque No	Details	Amount
28 July	PL03	Skipton & Co	170014	Invoice 1087	501.00
28 July	PL01	Radcliff & Sons	170015	Invoice 1099	660.00

TASK 14

The following payments were received from customers; enter the receipts on the accounts system.

Date	Customer	Cheque No	Details	Amount (£)
28 July	J Hollingham	087651	Invoice 1052	2675.52
28 July	Harry Bucket	198871	Invoice 1054	Part Payment of 500.00

TASK 15

On 14th July a member of staff buys a Tennis Racquet paying you £50.00 in Cash. This is inclusive of sales tax. Enter this in to the bank current account and use reference ST5 for the transaction.

TASK 16

On 19th July, you sold a 'Golf Club' to a customer and they paid £45.00 (Plus VAT) debit card. Use reference CS03.

TASK 17

A cheque you received from Kerry Jenkins for £758.34 (Cheque No 222547) has been returned by the bank marked 'Refer to Drawer – Insufficient Funds'. Process this returned cheque through the records, dated 12th July.

TASK 18

Refer to the following email below from Nina Birk

E-Mail
From: Nina Birk
Date: 31st July 20XX
Subject: Customer write off

Hello

In view of Paul McCallum, we have continuously chased this customer for payment and received no response. I have decided that we should write off the balance of their account at 31st July. Please ensure that this is done.

Thanks

Nina

TASK 19

You are given the following bank statement and are asked to produce a bank reconciliation at 31st July, processing any adjustments that may be necessary.

<table>
<tr><td colspan="4" align="center">**Sully Bank plc**</td></tr>
<tr><td colspan="4" align="center">201 Main Road</td></tr>
<tr><td colspan="4" align="center">Gillingham</td></tr>
<tr><td colspan="4" align="center">Kent</td></tr>
<tr><td colspan="4" align="center">ME3 5TF</td></tr>
</table>

Sports Gear
34 Hockey Avenue
Tennison   31st July 20XX
London   Statement no: 1001
EC1V 1NY

Account number 00678432

Statement of Account

Date: July 2011	Details	Paid out £	Paid in £	Balance £
01 July	Opening balance			3325.40C
12 July	Counter Credit		758.34	4083.74C
12 July	Dishonoured cheque	758.34		3325.40C
13 July	BACS		2767.34	6092.74C
13 July	Counter credit		1200.00	7292.74C
14 July	Counter credit		50.00	7342.74C
15 July	Counter credit		2879.40	10222.14C
15 July	Counter credit		1194.90	11417.04C
19 July	Cheque 170013	2801.00		8616.04C
20 July	Counter Credit		2849.37	11465.41C
20 July	Debit Card		54.00	11519.41C
25 July	Counter Debit	3441.00		8078.41C
29 July	Counter Credit		2675.52	10753.93C
29 July	Counter Credit		500.00	11253.93C
29 July	Standing Order – Ipswich Union	100.00		11153.93C
31 July	Bank charges	32.19		11121.74C
	D = Debit C = Credit			

TASK 20

Transfer £432.16 from the bank current account to the petty cash account. Use reference TRF01 for this transaction and date it 31st July.

TASK 21

Print out the following reports:

- Customer address list
- Period Trial Balance Report
- Sales Day Book
- Purchase Day Book
- Customer Activity Report (detailed)
- Supplier Activity Report (detailed)
- Nominal Ledger Activity Report for the following accounts
    - Bank Current Account
    - Petty Cash Account
- Aged Creditors Report
- Aged Debtors Report
- Print Statement for Paul McCallum
- Reconciliation (Reconciled transactions)

PRACTICE PAPER 5

WAY TO WORK LTD

THE SITUATION

This assignment is based on an existing business, Way to Work Ltd.

At the start of the business they operated under a manual bookkeeping system but they have now decided that from 1st March 20XX the accounting system will become computerised.

Some nominal ledger accounts have already been allocated suitable account codes. **You may need to amend or create other account codes.**

Way to Work's financial year starts in January.

Their company details are:-

Way to Work Ltd

55 Upper Street

London

N1 9PE

You are employed as an accounting technician.

The business is registered for VAT. The company's products are standard rated for VAT (20%).

Set the company's financial year to start in January 20XX

Today is 31st March in the current financial year.

TASK 1

Refer to the customer listing below and set up customer records to open Sales Ledger accounts for each customer.

Customer account code	Customer name, address and contact details	Customer account details
JP01	Morgan, Smith & Winston City Road Islington London N1 9PL	Credit limit: £7000 Payment Terms: 30 days Opening Balance: £1172.34 (relates to invoice INV021 dated 14th February 20XX)
JP02	Cyril West Grays West Grays Inn Road London WC1 1LT	Credit limit: £8500 Payment Terms: 30 days Opening Balance: £2954.00 (relates to invoice INV045 dated 22nd February 20XX).
JP03	Wallace & Gromit Ltd 134 Upper Street Islington London N1 2PT	Credit limit: £17000 Payment Terms: 30 days Opening Balance: £3180.00 (relates to invoice INV033 dated 18th February 20XX)
JP04	Star Paper 66 White Lion Street London N1 5RX	Credit limit: £12500 Payment Terms: 30 days Opening Balance: £1867.34 – relates to invoice INV34 dated 22nd February 20XX)

TASK 2

Refer to the supplier listing below and set up supplier records to open Purchase Ledger accounts for each supplier.

Supplier account code	Supplier name, address and contact details	Supplier account details
SP01	Paper Products UK South Down Trading Estate Sheffield S15 4DR	Credit limit: £8500 Payment Terms: 30 days Opening Balance: £445.23 – relates to invoice 0165 dated 28th February 20XX).
SP02	Wallace & Gromit Ltd 134 Upper Street Islington London N1 2PT	Credit limit: £12000 Payment Terms: 30 days Opening Balance: £6711.00 (relates to invoice 02183 dated 11th February 20XX)
SP03	Whole Office Furniture 176 East Way Leeds LD4 6PP	Credit limit: £4000 Payment Terms: 30 days Opening Balance: £1875.21 (relates to invoice 1028 dated 26th February 20XX)
SP04	Stationery World 32 Great Portland Road London WC1V 6HH	Credit limit: £16500 Payment Terms: 30 days Opening Balance: £9504.32 (relates to invoice 0187 dated 18th February 20XX).

TASK 3.1

Set up or amend the following nominal codes

Account number	Account name
4000	Stationery Sales
4001	CD Roms Sales
4002	Printer Accessory Sales
5000	Stationery Purchases
5001	CD Rom Purchases
5002	Printer Accessory Purchases
7005	Wages and Salaries
7803	General Expenses
3000	Capital
3260	Drawings

TASK 3.2

Refer to the list of General ledger balances below. Enter the opening balances into the computer, making sure you select the appropriate general ledger account codes.

List of general ledger balances as at 01.03.20XX

Account name	£	£
Motor Vehicle	14000.00	
Furniture and Fixtures	8000.00	
Bank	6210.81	
Petty Cash	100.00	
Sales Ledger Control Account *	9173.68	
Purchase Ledger Control Account*		18535.76
Capital		34000.00
Drawings	1000.00	
Stationery Sales		903.73
CD Roms Sales		855.00
Printer Accessories Sales		9842.00
Stationery purchases	2400.00	
CD Rom purchases	210.00	
Printer Accessory purchases	15000.00	
Wages and Salaries	5600.00	
General Expenses	342.00	
Rent	2100.00	
Note You do not need to enter these figures as you have already entered opening balances for customers and suppliers.		

TASK 3.2a

Transfer £1500.00 from the bank current account to the bank deposit account. Date the transaction 1st March and use reference TRANS01.

TASK 3.3

(a)   Print out the following reports and **identify and correct any errors**.

- Customer Address List
- Supplier Address List
- Period Trial Balance

TASK 4

(a)   Enter the sales invoices onto the computer.

Date	A/C No.	Invoice Ref	Description	Nominal Code	Gross £	VAT £	Net £
3 Mar	JP02	INV041	Stationery	4000	936.00	156.00	780.00
3 Mar	JP04	INV042	CD Roms	4001	1105.20	184.20	921.00
5 Mar	JP01	INV043	Printer Accessory	4002	5251.20	875.20	4376.00
7 Mar	JP03	INV044	Printer Accessory	4002	549.60	91.60	458.00
7 Mar	JP01	INV045	Stationery	4000	7452.00	1242.00	6210.00

(b)   On 17th March you send a credit note (CR51) to Star Paper (Account No JP04) for Printer Accessories.

The total is £251.27 plus tax.

TASK 5

(a)   Enter the purchases invoices into the computer.

Date	A/C No.	Invoice Ref	Description	Nominal Code	Gross	Vat	Net
10 Mar	SP01	0200	Stationery	5000	586.80	97.80	489.00
11 Mar	SP02	02241	CD Roms	5001	414.00	69.00	345.00
11 Mar	SP03	1098	Printer Accessory	5002	9153.60	1525.60	7628.00
14 Mar	SP04	0197	Stationery	5000	4280.40	713.40	3567.00

(b)   Enter the following purchase credit note onto the computer system.

Date	A/C No	Supplier	N/C	Credit Note Ref	Amount	Details
19 Mar	SP04	Stationery World	5000	RF287	124.08	Plus Tax

TASK 6

On the 28th March, a member of staff purchases a 'Printer Accessories' from you and pays you a total of £123.48 in cash. This is inclusive of VAT of £20.58. Use reference ST4 for this transaction and enter the funds in to the bank current account.

TASK 7

The following payments were received from customers; enter the receipts on the accounts system.

Date	Cheque Number	Customer	Amount	Details
15 Mar	203998	Morgan, Smith & Winston	1172.34	Payment for invoice INV021
17 Mar	103112	Cyril West	2954.00	Payment for invoice INV045
19 Mar	011211	Star Paper	1565.82	Payment for invoice INV034 including credit note CR51

TASK 8

The following cheque payments were sent to suppliers; enter the payments on the accounts system dated 31st March, and **raise the relevant remittance advices**.

Supplier	Cheque No:	Amount	Details
Paper Products UK	100076	445.23	Payment for invoice 0165
Whole Office Furniture	100077	1875.21	Payment for invoice 1028
Stationery World	100078	9504.32	Payment for invoice 0187

TASK 9

On the 31st March you are asked to set up a monthly standing order for Rent for £568.00 (Exempt VAT) for a period of 12 months commencing on 31st March. The Rent is payable to ICPW Bank. Process the payment for March.

TASK 10

Enter the following petty cash payments into the computer:

Date	Ref	Nominal Code	Details	Net	VAT	Gross
19 Mar	056	7200	Electricity	84.10	16.82	100.92
20 Mar	057	6201	Advertising	327.00	65.40	392.40

TASK 11

Enter the following journal into the computer:

JNL 001			
Date	Account name	Dr	Cr
19 Mar	Wages & Salaries	100.00	
20 Mar	General Expenses		100.00

TASK 12

(a)   On 15th March you transfer £600.00 from the Bank account to the Petty Cash account. Use reference TRANS02 for this transaction.

(b)   A cheque sent to Paper Products for £445.23 (cheque number 100076) has not been delivered to the supplier. Cancel this cheque through the records dated 31st March 20XX.

(c)   You are given the following bank statement and are asked to produce a bank reconciliation at 31st March, processing any adjustments that may be necessary.

<table>
<tr><td colspan="5" align="center">**Islington Bank Plc**</td></tr>
<tr><td colspan="5" align="center">201 Upper Street</td></tr>
<tr><td colspan="5" align="center">Islington</td></tr>
<tr><td colspan="5" align="center">London</td></tr>
<tr><td colspan="5" align="center">N1 9PE</td></tr>
</table>

Way to Work Ltd
55 Upper Street
London
N1 9PE

31st March 20XX

Statement no: 0002

Account number: 32543211

Statement of Account

Date: March 20XX	Details	Paid out £	Paid in £	Balance £
01 Mar	Opening balance			6210.81C
01 Mar	Transfer	1500.00		4710.81C
15 Mar	Transfer	600.00		4110.81C
18 Mar	Counter Credit		1172.34	5283.15C
18 Mar	Counter Credit		2954.00	8237.15C
19 Mar	Counter Credit		1565.82	9802.97C
23 Mar	Cancelled cheque		445.23	10248.20C
26 Mar	100017	1875.21		8372.99C
28 Mar	Counter credit		123.48	8496.47C
31 Mar	100076	445.23		8051.24C
31 Mar	Standing Order – ICPW Bank	568.00		7483.24C
31 Mar	Bank Charges	123.45		7359.79C
	D = Debit C = Credit			

TASK 13

Print the following reports:

- Customer Activity (detailed report)
- Supplier Activity (detailed report)
- Period Trial Balance for the month of March
- Audit Trail for March only
- Nominal Ledger Activity Report for the following accounts
  - Bank Current Account
  - Petty Cash Account
- Sales Day Book
- Purchases Day Book
- Aged Creditors
- Aged Debtors
- Statement for Cyril West
- Bank Reconciliation (Reconciled transactions)

Section 2

ANSWERS TO PRACTICE QUESTIONS

PRACTICE PAPER 1

TOY SHOP ANSWERS

TASK 3.4

Customer Address List

| Date: 22/08/2017 | | Toy Shop | | Page: 1 |
| Time: 18:45:33 | | Customer Address List | | |

Customer From:
Customer To: ZZZZZZZZ

A/C	Name & Address	Contact Name	Telephone	Fax
BB01	Busy Bee Toys 832 High Street Oxford OX2 3WG			
FF02	Forming Fun 21 Newton Quay Knott Mill Manchester M6 3RJ			
SM03	Space Models 13 Central Street Perth Scotland SC4 8RQ			
TP04	Teddy's T Party 3 Paradise Street Wokingham WO4 6QP			

Supplier Address List

Date:	22/08/2017	**Toy Shop**	Page:	1
Time:	18:47:58	**Supplier Address List**		

Supplier From:
Supplier To: ZZZZZZZZ

A/C	Name	Contact	Telephone	Fax
PL01	Abacus C & C Unit 31 Kitts Industrial Estate St Helens Lancs			
PL02	Compugames Ltd. 6 Jury Road Dublin Eire			
PL03	Space Models 13 Central Street Perth Scotland SC4 8RQ			
PL04	Toys Unlimited 95 Cuscaden Road Edinburgh Scotland			

Period Trial Balance Report

Date:	22/08/2017	**Toy Shop**	Page:	1
Time:	19:14:05	**Period Trial Balance**		

To Period: Month 2, May 2017

N/C	Name	Debit	Credit
0040	Furniture and Fixtures	5,800.00	
0050	Motor Vehicles	3,000.00	
1100	Debtors Control Account	2,223.60	
1200	Bank Current Account	3,725.00	
1210	Bank Deposit Account	500.00	
1230	Petty Cash	300.00	
2100	Creditors Control Account		2,157.60
2200	Sales Tax Control Account		543.00
2201	Purchase Tax Control Account	109.00	
3000	Capital		20,000.00
3260	Drawings	355.00	
4000	Sales - Computer Games		6,080.00
4001	Sales - Boxed Games		1,967.00
4002	Sales - Jigsaws		700.00
5000	Purchases - Computer Games	8,000.00	
5001	Purchases - Boxed Games	2,465.00	
5002	Purchases - Jigsaws	3,200.00	
7100	Rent and Rates	1,550.00	
7200	Electricity	167.00	
7504	Office Stationery	53.00	
	Totals:	31,447.60	31,447.60

TASK 8

Remittance advices

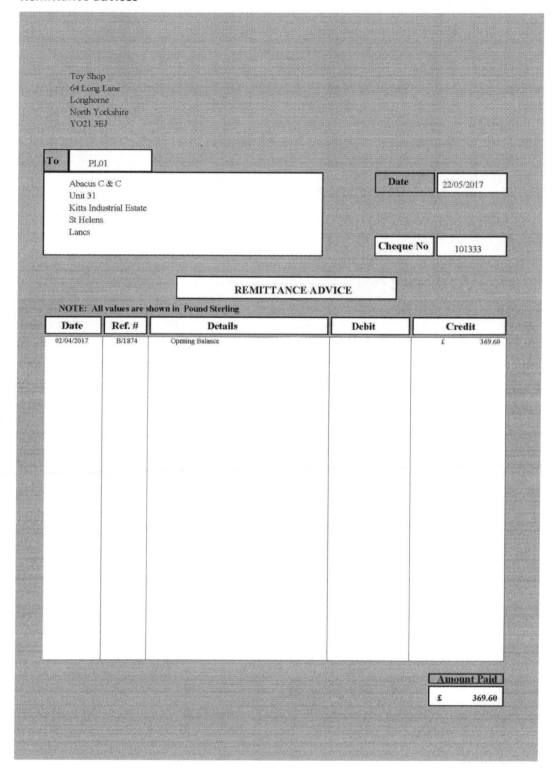

Toy Shop
64 Long Lane
Longhorne
North Yorkshire
YO21 3EJ

To	PL01

Abacus C & C
Unit 31
Kitts Industrial Estate
St Helens
Lancs

Date	22/05/2017

Cheque No	101333

REMITTANCE ADVICE

NOTE: All values are shown in Pound Sterling

Date	Ref. #	Details	Debit	Credit
02/04/2017	B/1874	Opening Balance		£ 369.60

Amount Paid	
£	369.60

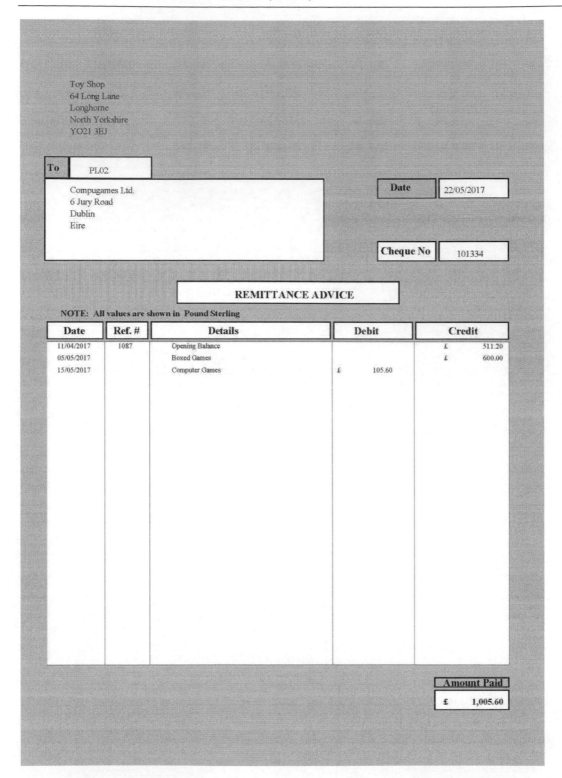

Toy Shop
64 Long Lane
Longhorne
North Yorkshire
YO21 3EJ

To	PL02		Date	22/05/2017

Compugames Ltd.
6 Jury Road
Dublin
Eire

	Cheque No	101334

REMITTANCE ADVICE

NOTE: All values are shown in Pound Sterling

Date	Ref. #	Details	Debit	Credit
11/04/2017	1087	Opening Balance		£ 511.20
05/05/2017		Boxed Games		£ 600.00
15/05/2017		Computer Games	£ 105.60	

Amount Paid
£ 1,005.60

TASK 9

Screen shot to show setting up the recurring entry

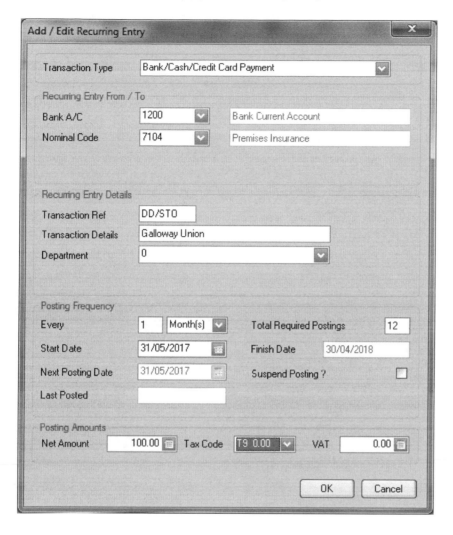

TASK 12

(a) Period Trial Balance Report

Date: 22/08/2017   **Toy Shop**   Page: 1
Time: 19:39:05   **Period Trial Balance**

To Period: Month 12, March 2018

N/C	Name	Debit	Credit
0040	Furniture and Fixtures	5,800.00	
0050	Motor Vehicles	3,000.00	
1100	Debtors Control Account	10,897.20	
1200	Bank Current Account	5,968.60	
1210	Bank Deposit Account	500.00	
1230	Petty Cash	255.52	
2100	Creditors Control Account		3,034.80
2200	Sales Tax Control Account		2,775.90
2201	Purchase Tax Control Account	483.48	
3000	Capital		20,000.00
3260	Drawings	2,355.00	
4000	Sales - Computer Games		15,340.00
4001	Sales - Boxed Games		4,866.50
4002	Sales - Jigsaws		700.00
5000	Purchases - Computer Games	9,362.00	
5001	Purchases - Boxed Games	2,965.00	
5002	Purchases - Jigsaws	3,218.00	
7100	Rent and Rates	1,550.00	
7104	Premises Insurance	100.00	
7200	Electricity	167.00	
7504	Office Stationery	53.00	
8201	Subscriptions	32.00	
8205	Refreshments	10.40	
	Totals:	46,717.20	46,717.20

(b) Sales Day Book

Date: 22/08/2017   **Toy Shop**   Page: 1
Time: 19:39:28   **Day Books: Customer Invoices (Detailed)**

Date From: 01/01/1980   Customer From:
Date To: 31/12/2019   Customer To: ZZZZZZZZ

Transaction From: 1   N/C From:
Transaction To: 99,999,999   N/C To: 99999999

Dept From: 0
Dept To: 999

Tran No.	Type	Date	A/C Ref	N/C	Inv Ref	Dept.	Details	Net Amount	Tax Amount	T/C	Gross Amount	V	B
1	SI	12/04/2017	BB01	9998	021	0	Opening Balance	349.20	0.00	T9	349.20	-	-
2	SI	08/04/2017	FF02	9998	035	0	Opening Balance	99.60	0.00	T9	99.60	-	-
3	SI	10/04/2017	SM03	9998	093	0	Opening Balance	1,195.20	0.00	T9	1,195.20	-	-
4	SI	17/04/2017	TP04	9998	1003	0	Opening Balance	579.60	0.00	T9	579.60	-	-
45	SI	04/05/2017	BB01	4000	2021	0	Computer Games	2,585.00	517.00	T1	3,102.00	N	-
46	SI	04/05/2017	FF02	4001	2022	0	Boxed Games	500.00	100.00	T1	600.00	N	-
47	SI	06/05/2017	TP04	4000	2023	0	Computer Games	5,000.00	1,000.00	T1	6,000.00	N	-
							Totals:	10,308.60	1,617.00		11,925.60		

(c) Sales Returns Day Book

Date:	22/08/2017		Toy Shop							Page:	1
Time:	19:39:54		**Day Books: Customer Credits (Detailed)**								

Date From:	01/01/1980				Customer From:	
Date To:	31/12/2019				Customer To:	ZZZZZZZZ
Transaction From:	1				N/C From:	
Transaction To:	99,999,999				N/C To:	99999999
Dept From:	0					
Dept To:	999					

Tran No.	Type	Date	A/C Ref	N/C	Inv Ref	Dept.	Details	Net Amount	Tax Amount	T/C	Gross Amount	V	B
48	SC	13/05/2017	TP04	4000	CN101	0	Return of faulty computer games	320.00	64.00	T1	384.00	N	-
							Totals:	320.00	64.00		384.00		

(d) Purchase Day Book

Date:	22/08/2017		Toy Shop							Page:	1
Time:	19:40:21		**Day Books: Supplier Invoices (Detailed)**								

Date From:	01/01/1980				Supplier From:	
Date To:	31/12/2019				Supplier To:	ZZZZZZZZ
Transaction From:	1				N/C From:	
Transaction To:	99,999,999				N/C To:	99999999
Dept From:	0					
Dept To:	999					

Tran No.	Type	Date	A/C Ref	N/C	Inv Ref	Dept	Details	Net Amount	Tax Amount	T/C	Gross Amount	V	B
5	PI	02/04/2017	PL01	9998	B/1874	0	Opening Balance	369.60	0.00	T9	369.60	-	-
6	PI	11/04/2017	PL02	9998	1087	0	Opening Balance	511.20	0.00	T9	511.20	-	-
7	PI	18/04/2017	PL03	9998	F-0193	0	Opening Balance	306.00	0.00	T9	306.00	-	-
8	PI	18/04/2017	PL04	9998	W/032	0	Opening Balance	970.80	0.00	T9	970.80	-	-
49	PI	03/05/2017	PL01	5000		0	Computer Games	450.00	90.00	T1	540.00	N	-
50	PI	05/05/2017	PL02	5001		0	Boxed Games	500.00	100.00	T1	600.00	N	-
51	PI	10/05/2017	PL03	5000		0	Computer Games	1,000.00	200.00	T1	1,200.00	N	-
52	PI	10/05/2017	PL04	5002		0	Jigsaws	18.00	0.00	T0	18.00	N	-
							Totals	4,125.60	390.00		4,515.60		

(e) Customer Activity Report

| Date: | 22/08/2017 | **Toy Shop** | | Page: | 1 |
| Time: | 19:40:53 | **Customer Activity (Detailed)** | | | |

Date From:	01/01/1980		Customer From:	
Date To:	22/08/2017		Customer To:	ZZZZZZZZ
Transaction From:	1		N/C From:	
Transaction To:	99,999,999		N/C To:	99999999
Inc b/fwd transaction:	No		Dept From:	0
Exc later payment:	No		Dept To:	999

** NOTE: All report values are shown in Base Currency, unless otherwise indicated **

A/C: BB01   Name: Busy Bee Toys   Contact: Tel:

No	Type	Date	Ref	N/C	Details	Dept	T/C	Value	O/S	Debit	Credit	V	B
1	SI	12/04/2017	021	9998	Opening Balance	0	T9	349.20		349.20		-	-
45	SI	04/05/2017	2021	4000	Computer Games	0	T1	3,102.00 *	3,102.00	3,102.00		N	-
57	SR	17/05/2017		1200	Sales Receipt	0	T9	349.20			349.20	-	N
					Totals:			3,102.00	3,102.00	3,451.20	349.20		

Amount Outstanding	3,102.00
Amount Paid this period	349.20
Credit Limit £	4,000.00
Turnover YTD	2,934.20

A/C: FF02   Name: Forming Fun   Contact: Tel:

No	Type	Date	Ref	N/C	Details	Dept	T/C	Value	O/S	Debit	Credit	V	B
2	SI	08/04/2017	035	9998	Opening Balance	0	T9	99.60		99.60		-	-
46	SI	04/05/2017	2022	4001	Boxed Games	0	T1	600.00 *	600.00	600.00		N	-
58	SR	17/05/2017		1200	Sales Receipt	0	T9	99.60			99.60	-	N
					Totals:			600.00	600.00	699.60	99.60		

Amount Outstanding	600.00
Amount Paid this period	99.60
Credit Limit £	4,000.00
Turnover YTD	599.60

A/C: SM03   Name: Space Models   Contact: Tel:

No	Type	Date	Ref	N/C	Details	Dept	T/C	Value	O/S	Debit	Credit	V	B
3	SI	10/04/2017	093	9998	Opening Balance	0	T9	1,195.20 *	1,195.20	1,195.20		-	-
					Totals:			1,195.20	1,195.20	1,195.20			

Amount Outstanding	1,195.20
Amount Paid this period	0.00
Credit Limit £	3,000.00
Turnover YTD	1,195.20

A/C: TP04   Name: Teddy's T Party   Contact: Tel:

No	Type	Date	Ref	N/C	Details	Dept	T/C	Value	O/S	Debit	Credit	V	B
4	SI	17/04/2017	1003	9998	Opening Balance	0	T9	579.60		579.60		-	-
47	SI	06/05/2017	2023	4000	Computer Games	0	T1	6,000.00 *	6,000.00	6,000.00		N	-
48	SC	13/05/2017	CN101	4000	Return of faulty computer games	0	T1	384.00			384.00	N	-
59	SR	26/05/2017		1200	Sales Receipt	0	T9	195.60			195.60	-	N
					Totals:			6,000.00	6,000.00	6,579.60	579.60		

Amount Outstanding	6,000.00
Amount Paid this period	195.60
Credit Limit £	7,000.00
Turnover YTD	5,259.60

(f) Supplier Activity Report

| Date: | 22/08/2017 | **Toy Shop** | Page: 1 |
| Time: | 19:41:23 | **Supplier Activity (Detailed)** | |

Date From:	01/01/1980		Supplier From:	
Date To:	22/08/2017		Supplier To:	ZZZZZZZZ
Transaction From:	1		N/C From:	
Transaction To:	99,999,999		N/C To:	99999999
Inc b/fwd transaction:	No		Dept From:	0
Exc later payment:	No		Dept To:	999

** NOTE: All report values are shown in Base Currency, unless otherwise indicated **

| A/C: | PL01 | Name: | Abacus C & C | | Contact: | | | Tel: | |

No	Type	Date	Ref	N/C	Details	Dept	T/C	Value	O/S	Debit	Credit	V	B
5	PI	02/04/2017	B/1874	9998	Opening Balance	0	T9	369.60	0.00		369.60	-	-
49	PI	03/05/2017		5000	Computer Games	0	T1	540.00 *	540.00		540.00	N	-
60	PP	22/05/2017	101333	1200	Purchase Payment	0	T9	369.60	0.00	369.60		-	N
					Totals:			540.00	540.00	369.60	909.60		

Amount Outstanding	540.00
Amount paid this period	369.60
Credit Limit £	5,500.00
Turnover YTD	819.60

| A/C: | PL02 | Name: | Compugames Ltd | | Contact: | | | Tel: | |

No	Type	Date	Ref	N/C	Details	Dept	T/C	Value	O/S	Debit	Credit	V	B
6	PI	11/04/2017	1087	9998	Opening Balance	0	T9	511.20	0.00		511.20	-	-
50	PI	05/05/2017		5001	Boxed Games	0	T1	600.00	0.00		600.00	N	-
53	PC	15/05/2017		5000	Computer Games	0	T1	105.60	0.00	105.60		N	-
61	PP	22/05/2017	101334	1200	Purchase Payment	0	T9	1,005.60	0.00	1,005.60		-	N
					Totals:			0.00	0.00	1,111.20	1,111.20		

Amount Outstanding	0.00
Amount paid this period	1,005.60
Credit Limit £	4,000.00
Turnover YTD	923.20

| A/C: | PL03 | Name: | Space Models | | Contact: | | | Tel: | |

No	Type	Date	Ref	N/C	Details	Dept	T/C	Value	O/S	Debit	Credit	V	B
7	PI	18/04/2017	F-0193	9998	Opening Balance	0	T9	306.00 *	306.00		306.00	-	-
51	PI	10/05/2017		5000	Computer Games	0	T1	1,200.00 *	1,200.00		1,200.00	N	-
					Totals:			1,506.00	1,506.00	0.00	1,506.00		

Amount Outstanding	1,506.00
Amount paid this period	0.00
Credit Limit £	2,000.00
Turnover YTD	1,306.00

| A/C: | PL04 | Name: | Toys Unlimited | | Contact: | | | Tel: | |

No	Type	Date	Ref	N/C	Details	Dept	T/C	Value	O/S	Debit	Credit	V	B
8	PI	18/04/2017	W/032	9998	Opening Balance	0	T9	970.80 *	970.80		970.80	-	-
52	PI	10/05/2017		5002	Jigsaws	0	T0	18.00 *	18.00		18.00	N	-
					Totals:			988.80	988.80	0.00	988.80		

Amount Outstanding	988.80
Amount paid this period	0.00
Credit Limit £	2,000.00
Turnover YTD	988.80

(g) Aged Creditors Report

| Date: | 22/08/2017 | | | **Toy Shop** | | | | Page: | 1 |

| Time: | 19:42:30 | | | **Aged Creditors Analysis (Detailed)** | | | | | |

| Date From: | 01/01/1980 | | | | | Supplier From: | |
| Date To: | 22/08/2017 | | | | | Supplier To: | ZZZZZZZZ |

Include future transactions: No
Exclude later payments: No

** NOTE: All report values are shown in Base Currency, unless otherwise indicated **

A/C:	PL01	Name:	Abacus C & C		Contact:				Tel:	

No:	Type	Date	Ref	Details	Balance	Future	Current	Period 1	Period 2	Period 3	Older
49	PI	03/05/2017		Computer Games	540.00	0.00	0.00	0.00	0.00	540.00	0.00
				Totals:	540.00	0.00	0.00	0.00	0.00	540.00	0.00

Turnover: 819.60
Credit Limit £ 5,500.00

A/C:	PL03	Name:	Space Models		Contact:				Tel:	

No:	Type	Date	Ref	Details	Balance	Future	Current	Period 1	Period 2	Period 3	Older
7	PI	18/04/2017	F-0193	Opening Balance	306.00	0.00	0.00	0.00	0.00	0.00	306.00
51	PI	10/05/2017		Computer Games	1,200.00	0.00	0.00	0.00	0.00	1,200.00	0.00
				Totals:	1,506.00	0.00	0.00	0.00	0.00	1,200.00	306.00

Turnover: 1,306.00
Credit Limit £ 2,000.00

A/C:	PL04	Name:	Toys Unlimited		Contact:				Tel:	

No:	Type	Date	Ref	Details	Balance	Future	Current	Period 1	Period 2	Period 3	Older
8	PI	18/04/2017	W/032	Opening Balance	970.80	0.00	0.00	0.00	0.00	0.00	970.80
52	PI	10/05/2017		Jigsaws	18.00	0.00	0.00	0.00	0.00	18.00	0.00
				Totals:	988.80	0.00	0.00	0.00	0.00	18.00	970.80

Turnover: 988.80
Credit Limit £ 2,000.00

| | | | | Grand Totals: | 3,034.80 | 0.00 | 0.00 | 0.00 | 0.00 | 1,758.00 | 1,276.80 |

(h) Aged Debtors Report

| Date: | 22/08/2017 | **Toy Shop** | Page: | 1 |
| Time: | 19:43:08 | **Aged Debtors Analysis (Detailed)** | | |

Date From:	01/01/1980		Customer From:	
Date To:	22/08/2017		Customer To:	ZZZZZZZZ
Include future transactions:	No			
Exclude later payments:	No			

** NOTE: All report values are shown in Base Currency, unless otherwise indicated **

| A/C: | BB01 | Name: | Busy Bee Toys | | Contact: | | | Tel: | | |

No	Type	Date	Ref	Details	Balance	Future	Current	Period 1	Period 2	Period 3	Older
45	SI	04/05/2017	2021	Computer Games	3,102.00	0.00	0.00	0.00	0.00	3,102.00	0.00
				Totals:	3,102.00	0.00	0.00	0.00	0.00	3,102.00	0.00

| Turnover: | 2,934.20 |
| Credit Limit £ | 4,000.00 |

| A/C: | FF02 | Name: | Forming Fun | | Contact: | | | Tel: | | |

No	Type	Date	Ref	Details	Balance	Future	Current	Period 1	Period 2	Period 3	Older
46	SI	04/05/2017	2022	Boxed Games	600.00	0.00	0.00	0.00	0.00	600.00	0.00
				Totals:	600.00	0.00	0.00	0.00	0.00	600.00	0.00

| Turnover: | 599.60 |
| Credit Limit £ | 4,000.00 |

| A/C: | SM03 | Name: | Space Models | | Contact: | | | Tel: | | |

No	Type	Date	Ref	Details	Balance	Future	Current	Period 1	Period 2	Period 3	Older
3	SI	10/04/2017	093	Opening Balance	1,195.20	0.00	0.00	0.00	0.00	0.00	1,195.20
				Totals:	1,195.20	0.00	0.00	0.00	0.00	0.00	1,195.20

| Turnover: | 1,195.20 |
| Credit Limit £ | 3,000.00 |

| A/C: | TP04 | Name: | Teddy's T Party | | Contact: | | | Tel: | | |

No	Type	Date	Ref	Details	Balance	Future	Current	Period 1	Period 2	Period 3	Older
47	SI	06/05/2017	2023	Computer Games	6,000.00	0.00	0.00	0.00	0.00	6,000.00	0.00
				Totals:	6,000.00	0.00	0.00	0.00	0.00	6,000.00	0.00

| Turnover: | 5,259.60 |
| Credit Limit £ | 7,000.00 |

| | | | | Grand Totals: | 10,897.20 | 0.00 | 0.00 | 0.00 | 0.00 | 9,702.00 | 1,195.20 |

(i) Journal Day Book

	Date:	22/08/2017					**Toy Shop**					Page:	1	
	Time:	19:43:52					**Day Books: Nominal Ledger**							

Date From:	01/01/1980	N/C From:	
Date To:	31/12/2019	N/C To:	99999999

Transaction From:	1	Dept From:	0
Transaction To:	99,999,999	Dept To:	999

No	Type	N/C	Date	Ref	Ex.Ref	Details	Dept	T/C	Debit	Credit	V	B
9	JD	0040	01/05/2017	O/Bal		Opening Balance	0	T9	5,800.00		-	-
10	JC	9998	01/05/2017	O/Bal		Opening Balance	0	T9		5,800.00	-	-
11	JD	0050	01/05/2017	O/Bal		Opening Balance	0	T9	3,000.00		-	-
12	JC	9998	01/05/2017	O/Bal		Opening Balance	0	T9		3,000.00	-	-
13	JD	1200	01/05/2017	O/Bal		Opening Balance	0	T9	4,225.00		-	-
14	JC	9998	01/05/2017	O/Bal		Opening Balance	0	T9		4,225.00	-	-
15	JD	1230	01/05/2017	O/Bal		Opening Balance	0	T9	300.00		-	-
16	JC	9998	01/05/2017	O/Bal		Opening Balance	0	T9		300.00	-	-
17	JC	2200	01/05/2017	O/Bal		Opening Balance	0	T9		543.00	-	-
18	JD	9998	01/05/2017	O/Bal		Opening Balance	0	T9	543.00		-	-
19	JD	2201	01/05/2017	O/Bal		Opening Balance	0	T9	109.00		-	-
20	JC	9998	01/05/2017	O/Bal		Opening Balance	0	T9		109.00	-	-
21	JC	3000	01/05/2017	O/Bal		Opening Balance	0	T9		20,000.00	-	-
22	JD	9998	01/05/2017	O/Bal		Opening Balance	0	T9	20,000.00		-	-
23	JD	3260	01/05/2017	O/Bal		Opening Balance	0	T9	355.00		-	-
24	JC	9998	01/05/2017	O/Bal		Opening Balance	0	T9		355.00	-	-
25	JC	4000	01/05/2017	O/Bal		Opening Balance	0	T9		6,080.00	-	-
26	JD	9998	01/05/2017	O/Bal		Opening Balance	0	T9	6,080.00		-	-
27	JC	4002	01/05/2017	O/Bal		Opening Balance	0	T9		700.00	-	-
28	JD	9998	01/05/2017	O/Bal		Opening Balance	0	T9	700.00		-	-
29	JC	4001	01/05/2017	O/Bal		Opening Balance	0	T9		1,967.00	-	-
30	JD	9998	01/05/2017	O/Bal		Opening Balance	0	T9	1,967.00		-	-
31	JD	5000	01/05/2017	O/Bal		Opening Balance	0	T9	8,000.00		-	-
32	JC	9998	01/05/2017	O/Bal		Opening Balance	0	T9		8,000.00	-	-
33	JD	5002	01/05/2017	O/Bal		Opening Balance	0	T9	3,200.00		-	-
34	JC	9998	01/05/2017	O/Bal		Opening Balance	0	T9		3,200.00	-	-
35	JD	5001	01/05/2017	O/Bal		Opening Balance	0	T9	2,465.00		-	-
36	JC	9998	01/05/2017	O/Bal		Opening Balance	0	T9		2,465.00	-	-
37	JD	7504	01/05/2017	O/Bal		Opening Balance	0	T9	53.00		-	-
38	JC	9998	01/05/2017	O/Bal		Opening Balance	0	T9		53.00	-	-
39	JD	7200	01/05/2017	O/Bal		Opening Balance	0	T9	167.00		-	-
40	JC	9998	01/05/2017	O/Bal		Opening Balance	0	T9		167.00	-	-
41	JD	7100	01/05/2017	O/Bal		Opening Balance	0	T9	1,550.00		-	-
42	JC	9998	01/05/2017	O/Bal		Opening Balance	0	T9		1,550.00	-	-
43	JC	1200	01/05/2017	TRANS01		Bank Transfer	0	T9		500.00	-	N
44	JD	1210	01/05/2017	TRANS01		Bank Transfer	0	T9	500.00			N
65	JD	3260	25/05/2017	JNL02		Transfer of cash for James	0	T9	2,000.00		-	-
66	JC	1200	25/05/2017	JNL02		James Free's personal use	0	T9		2,000.00	-	N
								Totals:	61,014.00	61,014.00		

TASK 13

Customer record with new address

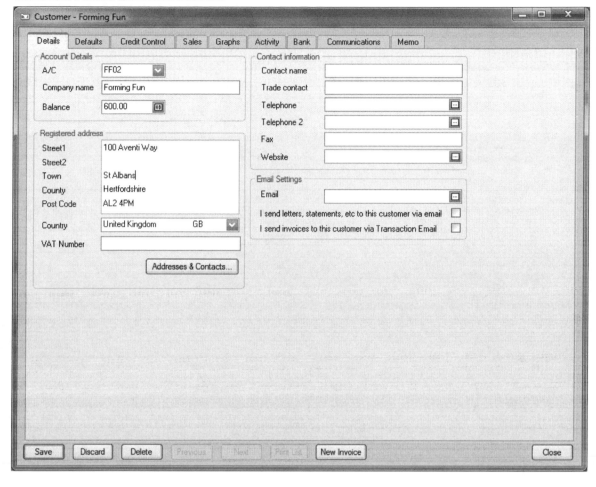

TASK 15

Remittance advices

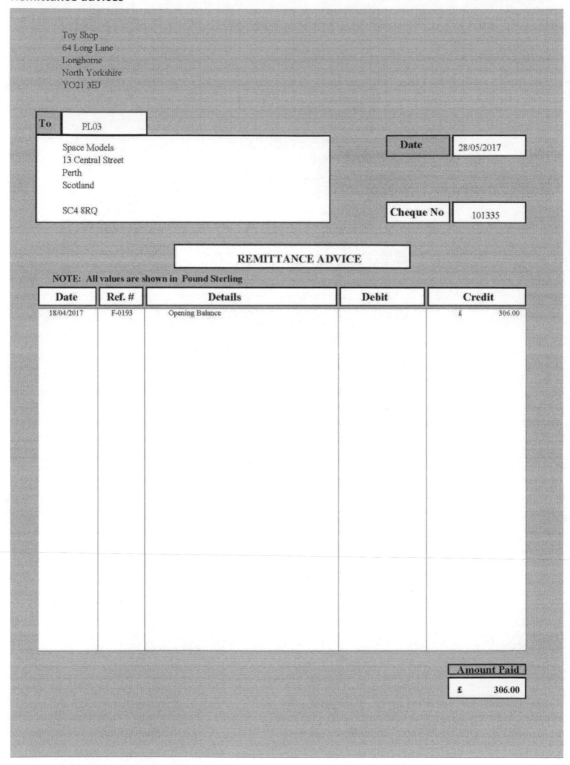

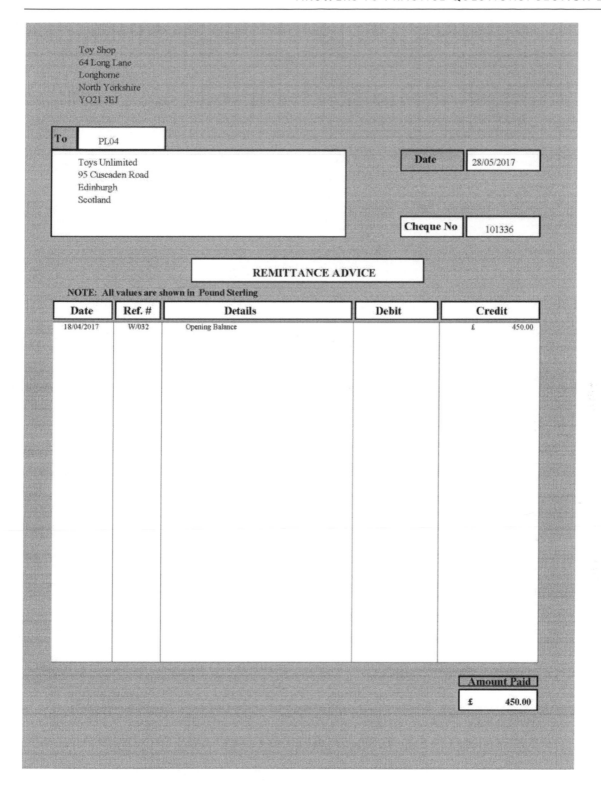

Toy Shop
64 Long Lane
Longhorne
North Yorkshire
YO21 3EJ

To	PL04

Toys Unlimited
95 Cuscaden Road
Edinburgh
Scotland

Date	28/05/2017

Cheque No	101336

REMITTANCE ADVICE

NOTE: All values are shown in Pound Sterling

Date	Ref. #	Details	Debit	Credit
18/04/2017	W/032	Opening Balance		£ 450.00

Amount Paid
£   450.00

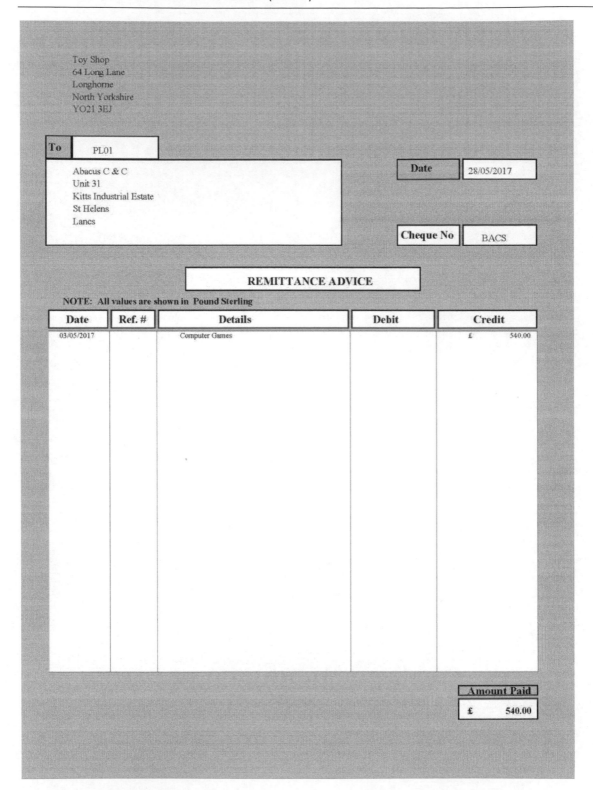

Toy Shop
64 Long Lane
Longhorne
North Yorkshire
YO21 3EJ

To	PL01

Abacus C & C
Unit 31
Kitts Industrial Estate
St Helens
Lancs

Date	28/05/2017

Cheque No	BACS

REMITTANCE ADVICE

NOTE: All values are shown in Pound Sterling

Date	Ref. #	Details	Debit	Credit
03/05/2017		Computer Games		£ 540.00

Amount Paid	
£	540.00

TASK 23

(a) Customer Activity (detailed) Report

Date:	22/08/2017		**Toy Shop**			Page:	1
Time:	20:36:17		**Customer Activity (Detailed)**				

Date From:	01/01/1980	Customer From:	
Date To:	22/08/2017	Customer To:	ZZZZZZZZ
Transaction From:	1	N/C From:	
Transaction To:	99,999,999	N/C To:	99999999
Inc b/fwd transaction:	No	Dept From:	0
Exc later payment:	No	Dept To:	999

** NOTE: All report values are shown in Base Currency, unless otherwise indicated **

A/C:	BB01	Name:		Busy Bee Toys		Contact:				Tel:				
No	**Type**	**Date**	**Ref**	**N/C**	**Details**	**Dept**	**T/C**	**Value**	**O/S**	**Debit**	**Credit**	**V**	**B**
1	SI	12/04/2017	021	9998	Opening Balance	0	T9	349.20		349.20		-	-
45	SI	04/05/2017	2021	4000	Computer Games	0	T1	3,102.00		3,102.00		N	-
57	SR	17/05/2017		1200	Sales Receipt	0	T9	349.20			349.20	-	R
79	SR	29/05/2017		1200	Sales Receipt	0	T9	3,102.00			3,102.00	-	R
					Totals:			0.00	0.00	3,451.20	3,451.20		

Amount Outstanding	0.00
Amount Paid this period	3,451.20
Credit Limit £	4,000.00
Turnover YTD	2,934.20

A/C:	FF02	Name:		Forming Fun		Contact:				Tel:				
No	**Type**	**Date**	**Ref**	**N/C**	**Details**	**Dept**	**T/C**	**Value**	**O/S**	**Debit**	**Credit**	**V**	**B**
2	SI	08/04/2017	035	9998	Opening Balance	0	T9	99.60		99.60		-	-
46	SI	04/05/2017	2022	4001	Boxed Games	0	T1	600.00 p	200.00	600.00		N	-
58	SR	17/05/2017	CANCEL	1200	Sales Receipt	0	T9	99.60			99.60	-	R
74	SP	17/05/2017	CANCEL	1200	Cancelled Cheque	0	T9	99.60	99.60	99.60		-	R
80	SR	29/05/2017		1200	Sales Receipt	0	T9	400.00			400.00	-	R
					Totals:			299.60	299.60	799.20	499.60		

Amount Outstanding	299.60
Amount Paid this period	400.00
Credit Limit £	4,000.00
Turnover YTD	599.60

A/C:	SM03	Name:		Space Models		Contact:				Tel:				
No	**Type**	**Date**	**Ref**	**N/C**	**Details**	**Dept**	**T/C**	**Value**	**O/S**	**Debit**	**Credit**	**V**	**B**
3	SI	10/04/2017	093	9998	Opening Balance	0	T9	1,195.20 *	1,195.20	1,195.20		-	-
					Totals:			1,195.20	1,195.20	1,195.20			

Amount Outstanding	1,195.20
Amount Paid this period	0.00
Credit Limit £	3,000.00
Turnover YTD	1,195.20

A/C:	TP04	Name:		Teddy's T Party		Contact:				Tel:				
No	**Type**	**Date**	**Ref**	**N/C**	**Details**	**Dept**	**T/C**	**Value**	**O/S**	**Debit**	**Credit**	**V**	**B**
4	SI	17/04/2017	1003	9998	Opening Balance	0	T9	579.60		579.60		-	-
47	SI	06/05/2017	2023	4000	Computer Games	0	T1	6,000.00		6,000.00		N	-
48	SC	13/05/2017	CN101	4000	Return of faulty computer games	0	T1	384.00			384.00	N	-
59	SR	26/05/2017		1200	Sales Receipt	0	T9	195.60			195.60	-	R
81	SR	29/05/2017		1200	Sales Receipt	0	T9	6,000.00			6,000.00	-	R
					Totals:			0.00	0.00	6,579.60	6,579.60		

Amount Outstanding	0.00
Amount Paid this period	6,195.60
Credit Limit £	7,000.00
Turnover YTD	5,259.60

(b) Supplier Activity (detailed) Report

| Date: | 22/08/2017 | **Toy Shop** | Page: | 1 |
| Time: | 20:36:48 | **Supplier Activity (Detailed)** | | |

Date From:	01/01/1980		Supplier From:	
Date To:	22/08/2017		Supplier To:	ZZZZZZZZ
Transaction From:	1		N/C From:	
Transaction To:	99,999,999		N/C To:	99999999
Inc b/fwd transaction:	No		Dept From:	0
Exc later payment:	No		Dept To:	999

** NOTE: All report values are shown in Base Currency, unless otherwise indicated **

A/C:	PL01	Name:	Abacus C & C		Contact:			Tel:			

No	Type	Date	Ref	N/C	Details	Dept	T/C	Value	O/S	Debit	Credit	V	B
5	PI	02/04/2017	B/1874	9998	Opening Balance	0	T9	369.60	0.00		369.60	-	-
49	PI	03/05/2017		5000	Computer Games	0	T1	540.00	0.00		540.00	N	-
60	PP	22/05/2017	101333	1200	Purchase Payment	0	T9	369.60	0.00	369.60		-	R
71	PP	28/05/2017	BACS	1200	Purchase Payment	0	T9	540.00	0.00	540.00		-	R
					Totals:			0.00	0.00	909.60	909.60		

Amount Outstanding	0.00
Amount paid this period	909.60
Credit Limit £	5,500.00
Turnover YTD	819.60

A/C:	PL02	Name:	Compugames Ltd.		Contact:			Tel:			

No	Type	Date	Ref	N/C	Details	Dept	T/C	Value	O/S	Debit	Credit	V	B
6	PI	11/04/2017	1087	9998	Opening Balance	0	T9	511.20	0.00		511.20	-	-
50	PI	05/05/2017		5001	Boxed Games	0	T1	600.00	0.00		600.00	N	-
53	PC	15/05/2017		5000	Computer Games	0	T1	105.60	0.00	105.60		N	-
61	PP	22/05/2017	101334	1200	Purchase Payment	0	T9	1,005.60	0.00	1,005.60		-	R
					Totals:			0.00	0.00	1,111.20	1,111.20		

Amount Outstanding	0.00
Amount paid this period	1,005.60
Credit Limit £	4,000.00
Turnover YTD	923.20

A/C:	PL03	Name:	Space Models		Contact:			Tel:			

No	Type	Date	Ref	N/C	Details	Dept	T/C	Value	O/S	Debit	Credit	V	B
7	PI	18/04/2017	F-0193	9998	Opening Balance	0	T9	306.00	0.00		306.00	-	-
51	PI	10/05/2017		5000	Computer Games	0	T1	1,200.00 *	1,200.00		1,200.00	N	-
69	PP	28/05/2017	101335	1200	Purchase Payment	0	T9	306.00	0.00	306.00		-	N
					Totals:			1,200.00	1,200.00	306.00	1,506.00		

Amount Outstanding	1,200.00
Amount paid this period	306.00
Credit Limit £	2,000.00
Turnover YTD	1,306.00

A/C:	PL04	Name:	Toys Unlimited		Contact:			Tel:			

No	Type	Date	Ref	N/C	Details	Dept	T/C	Value	O/S	Debit	Credit	V	B
8	PI	18/04/2017	W/032	9998	Opening Balance	0	T9	970.80 p	520.80		970.80	-	-
52	PI	10/05/2017		5002	Jigsaws	0	T0	18.00 *	18.00		18.00	N	-
70	PP	28/05/2017	101336	1200	Purchase Payment	0	T9	450.00	0.00	450.00		-	R
					Totals:			538.80	538.80	450.00	988.80		

Amount Outstanding	538.80
Amount paid this period	450.00
Credit Limit £	2,000.00
Turnover YTD	988.80

(c) Period Trial Balance for May

Date:	22/08/2017		**Toy Shop**	Page:	1
Time:	20:37:39		**Period Trial Balance**		

To Period: Month 12, March 2018

N/C	Name	Debit	Credit
0040	Furniture and Fixtures	5,800.00	
0050	Motor Vehicles	3,000.00	
1100	Debtors Control Account	1,494.80	
1200	Bank Current Account	24,238.20	
1210	Bank Deposit Account	500.00	
1230	Petty Cash	300.00	
2100	Creditors Control Account		1,738.80
2200	Sales Tax Control Account		2,819.90
2201	Purchase Tax Control Account	483.48	
2300	Loans		10,000.00
3000	Capital		20,000.00
3260	Drawings	2,355.00	
4000	Sales - Computer Games		15,560.00
4001	Sales - Boxed Games		4,866.50
4002	Sales - Jigsaws		745.00
5000	Purchases - Computer Games	9,362.00	
5001	Purchases - Boxed Games	2,965.00	
5002	Purchases - Jigsaws	3,218.00	
7100	Rent and Rates	1,048.00	
7104	Premises Insurance	100.00	
7200	Electricity	167.00	
7201	Gas	502.00	
7504	Office Stationery	53.00	
7901	Bank Charges	101.32	
8201	Subscriptions	32.00	
8205	Refreshments	10.40	
	Totals:	55,730.20	55,730.20

(d) Audit Trail for May (detailed – transactions only)

Date:	22/08/2017			**Toy Shop**					Page:	1
Time:	20:38:01			**Audit Trail (Detailed)**						

Date From:	01/01/1980		Customer From:	
Date To:	31/12/2019		Customer To:	ZZZZZZZZ
Transaction From:	1		Supplier From:	
Transaction To:	99,999,999		Supplier To:	ZZZZZZZZ

Exclude Deleted Tran: No

No	Type	A/C	N/C	Dept	Details	Date	Ref	Net	Tax	T/C	Pd	Paid	V	B	Bank Rec. Date
1	SI	BB01				12/04/2017	021	349.20	0.00		Y	349.20	-		
		1	9998	0	Opening Balance			349.20	0.00	T9		349.20	-		
					349.20 from SR 57	17/05/2017						349.20			
2	SI	FF02				08/04/2017	035	99.60	0.00		Y	99.60	-		
		2	9998	0	Opening Balance			99.60	0.00	T9		99.60	-		
					99.60 from SR 58	17/05/2017						99.60			
3	SI	SM03				10/04/2017	093	1,195.20	0.00		N	0.00	-		
		3	9998	0	Opening Balance			1,195.20	0.00	T9		0.00	-		
4	SI	TP04				17/04/2017	1003	579.60	0.00		Y	579.60	-		
		4	9998	0	Opening Balance			579.60	0.00	T9		579.60	-		
					384.00 from SC 48	13/05/2017	CN101					384.00			
					195.60 from SR 59	26/05/2017						195.60			
5	PI	PL01				02/04/2017	B/1874	369.60	0.00		Y	369.60	-		
		5	9998	0	Opening Balance			369.60	0.00	T9		369.60	-		
					369.60 from PP 60	22/05/2017	101333					369.60			
6	PI	PL02				11/04/2017	1087	511.20	0.00		Y	511.20	-		
		6	9998	0	Opening Balance			511.20	0.00	T9		511.20	-		
					105.60 from PC 53	15/05/2017						105.60			
					405.60 from PP 61	22/05/2017	101334					405.60			
7	PI	PL03				18/04/2017	F-0193	306.00	0.00		Y	306.00	-		
		7	9998	0	Opening Balance			306.00	0.00	T9		306.00	-		
					306.00 from PP 69	28/05/2017	101335					306.00			
8	PI	PL04				18/04/2017	W/032	970.80	0.00		N	450.00	-		
		8	9998	0	Opening Balance			970.80	0.00	T9		450.00	-		
					450.00 from PP 70	28/05/2017	101336					450.00			

| Date: | 22/08/2017 | | | | | | | **Toy Shop** | | | | | | | Page: 2 |
| Time: | 20:38:01 | | | | | | | **Audit Trail (Detailed)** | | | | | | | |

No	Type	A/C	N/C	Dept	Details	Date	Ref	Net	Tax	T/C	Pd	Paid	V	B	Bank Rec. Date
9	JD	0040				01/05/2017	O/Bal	5,800.00	0.00		Y	5,800.00	-		
		9	0040	0	Opening Balance			5,800.00	0.00	T9		5,800.00	-		
10	JC	9998				01/05/2017	O/Bal	5,800.00	0.00		Y	5,800.00	-		
		10	9998	0	Opening Balance			5,800.00	0.00	T9		5,800.00	-		
11	JD	0050				01/05/2017	O/Bal	3,000.00	0.00		Y	3,000.00	-		
		11	0050	0	Opening Balance			3,000.00	0.00	T9		3,000.00	-		
12	JC	9998				01/05/2017	O/Bal	3,000.00	0.00		Y	3,000.00	-		
		12	9998	0	Opening Balance			3,000.00	0.00	T9		3,000.00	-		
13	JD	1200				01/05/2017	O/Bal	4,225.00	0.00		Y	4,225.00	-		31/05/2017
		13	1200	0	Opening Balance			4,225.00	0.00	T9		4,225.00	-		
14	JC	9998				01/05/2017	O/Bal	4,225.00	0.00		Y	4,225.00	-		
		14	9998	0	Opening Balance			4,225.00	0.00	T9		4,225.00	-		
15	JD	1230				01/05/2017	O/Bal	300.00	0.00		Y	300.00	-		31/05/2017
		15	1230	0	Opening Balance			300.00	0.00	T9		300.00	-		
16	JC	9998				01/05/2017	O/Bal	300.00	0.00		Y	300.00	-		
		16	9998	0	Opening Balance			300.00	0.00	T9		300.00	-		
17	JC	2200				01/05/2017	O/Bal	543.00	0.00		Y	543.00	-		
		17	2200	0	Opening Balance			543.00	0.00	T9		543.00	-		
18	JD	9998				01/05/2017	O/Bal	543.00	0.00		Y	543.00	-		
		18	9998	0	Opening Balance			543.00	0.00	T9		543.00	-		
19	JD	2201				01/05/2017	O/Bal	109.00	0.00		Y	109.00	-		
		19	2201	0	Opening Balance			109.00	0.00			109.00	-		
20	JC	9998				01/05/2017	O/Bal	109.00	0.00		Y	109.00	-		
		20	9998	0	Opening Balance			109.00	0.00			109.00	-		
21	JC	3000				01/05/2017	O/Bal	20,000.00	0.00		Y	20,000.00	-		
		21	3000	0	Opening Balance			20,000.00	0.00	T9		20,000.00	-		
22	JD	9998				01/05/2017	O/Bal	20,000.00	0.00		Y	20,000.00	-		
		22	9998	0	Opening Balance			20,000.00	0.00	T9		20,000.00	-		
23	JD	3260				01/05/2017	O/Bal	355.00	0.00		Y	355.00	-		

| Date: | 22/08/2017 | | | | | | | **Toy Shop** | | | | | | | Page: 3 |
| Time: | 20:38:01 | | | | | | | **Audit Trail (Detailed)** | | | | | | | |

No	Type	A/C	N/C	Dept	Details	Date	Ref	Net	Tax	T/C	Pd	Paid	V	B	Bank Rec. Date
		23	3260	0	Opening Balance			355.00	0.00	T9		355.00	-		
24	JC	9998				01/05/2017	O/Bal	355.00	0.00		Y	355.00	-		
		24	9998	0	Opening Balance			355.00	0.00	T9		355.00	-		
25	JC	4000				01/05/2017	O/Bal	6,080.00	0.00		Y	6,080.00	-		
		25	4000	0	Opening Balance			6,080.00	0.00	T9		6,080.00	-		
26	JD	9998				01/05/2017	O/Bal	6,080.00	0.00		Y	6,080.00	-		
		26	9998	0	Opening Balance			6,080.00	0.00	T9		6,080.00	-		
27	JC	4002				01/05/2017	O/Bal	700.00	0.00		Y	700.00	-		
		27	4002	0	Opening Balance			700.00	0.00	T9		700.00	-		
28	JD	9998				01/05/2017	O/Bal	700.00	0.00		Y	700.00	-		
		28	9998	0	Opening Balance			700.00	0.00	T9		700.00	-		
29	JC	4001				01/05/2017	O/Bal	1,967.00	0.00		Y	1,967.00	-		
		29	4001	0	Opening Balance			1,967.00	0.00	T9		1,967.00	-		
30	JD	9998				01/05/2017	O/Bal	1,967.00	0.00		Y	1,967.00	-		
		30	9998	0	Opening Balance			1,967.00	0.00	T9		1,967.00	-		
31	JD	5000				01/05/2017	O/Bal	8,000.00	0.00		Y	8,000.00	-		
		31	5000	0	Opening Balance			8,000.00	0.00	T9		8,000.00	-		
32	JC	9998				01/05/2017	O/Bal	8,000.00	0.00		Y	8,000.00	-		
		32	9998	0	Opening Balance			8,000.00	0.00	T9		8,000.00	-		
33	JD	5002				01/05/2017	O/Bal	3,200.00	0.00		Y	3,200.00	-		
		33	5002	0	Opening Balance			3,200.00	0.00	T9		3,200.00	-		
34	JC	9998				01/05/2017	O/Bal	3,200.00	0.00		Y	3,200.00	-		
		34	9998	0	Opening Balance			3,200.00	0.00	T9		3,200.00	-		
35	JD	5001				01/05/2017	O/Bal	2,465.00	0.00		Y	2,465.00	-		
		35	5001	0	Opening Balance			2,465.00	0.00	T9		2,465.00	-		
36	JC	9998				01/05/2017	O/Bal	2,465.00	0.00		Y	2,465.00	-		
		36	9998	0	Opening Balance			2,465.00	0.00	T9		2,465.00	-		
37	JD	7504				01/05/2017	O/Bal	53.00	0.00		Y	53.00	-		
		37	7504	0	Opening Balance			53.00	0.00	T9		53.00	-		

Date: 22/08/2017
Time: 20:38:01

Toy Shop
Audit Trail (Detailed)

Page: 4

No	Type	A/C	N/C	Dept	Details	Date	Ref	Net	Tax	T/C	Pd	Paid	V	B	Bank Rec. Date
38	JC	9998				01/05/2017	O/Bal	53.00	0.00		Y	53.00	-		
		38	9998	0	Opening Balance			53.00	0.00	T9		53.00	-		
39	JD	7200				01/05/2017	O/Bal	167.00	0.00		Y	167.00	-		
		39	7200	0	Opening Balance			167.00	0.00	T9		167.00	-		
40	JC	9998				01/05/2017	O/Bal	167.00	0.00		Y	167.00	-		
		40	9998	0	Opening Balance			167.00	0.00	T9		167.00	-		
41	JD	7100				01/05/2017	O/Bal	1,550.00	0.00		Y	1,550.00	-		
		41	7100	0	Opening Balance			1,550.00	0.00	T9		1,550.00	-		
42	JC	9998				01/05/2017	O/Bal	1,550.00	0.00		Y	1,550.00	-		
		42	9998	0	Opening Balance			1,550.00	0.00	T9		1,550.00	-		
43	JC	1200				01/05/2017	TRANS01	500.00	0.00		Y	500.00	R		31/05/2017
		43	1200	0	Bank Transfer			500.00	0.00	T9		500.00	-		
44	JD	1210				01/05/2017	TRANS01	500.00	0.00		Y	500.00	N		
		44	1210	0	Bank Transfer			500.00	0.00	T9		500.00	-		
45	SI	BB01				04/05/2017	2021	2,585.00	517.00		Y	3,102.00	-		
		45	4000	0	Computer Games			2,585.00	517.00	T1		3,102.00	N		
					3102.00 from SR 79	29/05/2017						3,102.00			
46	SI	FF02				04/05/2017	2022	500.00	100.00		N	400.00	-		
		46	4001	0	Boxed Games			500.00	100.00	T1		400.00	N		
					400.00 from SR 80	29/05/2017						400.00			
47	SI	TP04				06/05/2017	2023	5,000.00	1,000.00		Y	6,000.00	-		
		47	4000	0	Computer Games			5,000.00	1,000.00	T1		6,000.00	N		
					6000.00 from SR 81	29/05/2017						6,000.00			
48	SC	TP04				13/05/2017	CN101	320.00	64.00		Y	384.00	-		
		48	4000	0	Return of faulty			320.00	64.00	T1		384.00	N		
					384.00 to SI 4	13/05/2017	1003					384.00			
49	PI	PL01				03/05/2017		450.00	90.00		Y	540.00	-		
		49	5000	0	Computer Games			450.00	90.00	T1		540.00	N		
					540.00 from PP 71	28/05/2017	BACS					540.00			
50	PI	PL02				05/05/2017		500.00	100.00		Y	600.00	-		

Date: 22/08/2017
Time: 20:38:01

Toy Shop
Audit Trail (Detailed)

Page: 5

No	Type	A/C	N/C	Dept	Details	Date	Ref	Net	Tax	T/C	Pd	Paid	V	B	Bank Rec. Date
		50	5001	0	Boxed Games			500.00	100.00	T1		600.00	N		
					600.00 from PP 61	22/05/2017	101334					600.00			
51	PI	PL03				10/05/2017		1,000.00	200.00		N	0.00	-		
		51	5000	0	Computer Games			1,000.00	200.00	T1		0.00	N		
52	PI	PL04				10/05/2017		18.00	0.00		N	0.00	-		
		52	5002	0	Jigsaws			18.00	0.00	T0		0.00	N		
53	PC	PL02				15/05/2017		88.00	17.60		Y	105.60	-		
		53	5000	0	Computer Games			88.00	17.60	T1		105.60	N		
					105.60 to PI 6	15/05/2017	1087					105.60			
54	BR	1200				13/05/2017	Cash Sales	3,399.50	679.90		Y	4,079.40	R		31/05/2017
		54	4000	0	Computer Games			1,000.00	200.00	T1		1,200.00	N		
		55	4001	0	Boxed Games			2,399.50	479.90	T1		2,879.40	N		
56	BR	1200				20/05/2017	Cash Sales	995.00	0.00		Y	995.00	R		31/05/2017
		56	4000	0	Computer Games			995.00	0.00	T0		995.00	N		
57	SR	BB01				17/05/2017		349.20	0.00		Y	349.20	R		31/05/2017
		57	1200	0	Sales Receipt			349.20	0.00	T9		349.20	-		
					349.20 to SI 1	17/05/2017	021					349.20			
58	SR	FF02				17/05/2017	CANCEL	99.60	0.00		Y	99.60	R		31/05/2017
		58	1200	0	Sales Receipt			99.60	0.00	T9		99.60	-		
					99.60 to SI 2	17/05/2017	035					99.60			
59	SR	TP04				26/05/2017		195.60	0.00		Y	195.60	R		31/05/2017
		59	1200	0	Sales Receipt			195.60	0.00	T9		195.60	-		
					195.60 to SI 4	26/05/2017	1003					195.60			
60	PP	PL01				22/05/2017	101333	369.60	0.00		Y	369.60	R		31/05/2017
		60	1200	0	Purchase Payment			369.60	0.00	T9		369.60	-		
					369.60 to PI 5	22/05/2017	B/1874					369.60			
61	PP	PL02				22/05/2017	101334	1,005.60	0.00		Y	1,005.60	R		31/05/2017
		61	1200	0	Purchase Payment			1,005.60	0.00	T9		1,005.60	-		
					405.60 to PI 6	22/05/2017	1087					405.60			
					600.00 to PI 50	22/05/2017						600.00			
62	BP	1200				31/05/2017	DD/STO	100.00	0.00		Y	100.00	R		31/05/2017

Date: 22/08/2017 Time: 20:38:01								Toy Shop Audit Trail (Detailed)						Page: 6
No	**Type**	**A/C**	**N/C**	**Dept**	**Details**	**Date**	**Ref**	**Net**	**Tax**	**T/C**	**Pd**	**Paid**	**V**	**B**	**Bank Rec. Date**
		62	7104	0	Galloway Union			100.00	0.00	T9		100.00		-	
63	CP	1230				20/05/2017	012	32.00	0.00		Y	32.00		-	
		63	8201	0	Subscriptions			32.00	0.00	T9		32.00		-	
64	CP	1230				21/05/2017	013	10.40	2.08		Y	12.48		-	
		64	8205	0	Refreshments			10.40	2.08	T1		12.48		N	
65	JD	3260				25/05/2017	JNL02	2,000.00	0.00		Y	2,000.00		-	
		65	3260	0	Transfer of cash for			2,000.00	0.00	T9		2,000.00		-	
66	JC	1200				25/05/2017	JNL02	2,000.00	0.00		Y	2,000.00		R	31/05/2017
		66	1200	0	James Free's			2,000.00	0.00	T9		2,000.00		-	
67	JD	7201				31/05/2017	JNL03	502.00	0.00		Y	502.00		-	
		67	7201	0	Being the transfer of			502.00	0.00	T9		502.00		-	
68	JC	7100				31/05/2017	JNL03	502.00	0.00		Y	502.00		-	
		68	7100	0	Being the transfer of			502.00	0.00	T9		502.00		-	
69	PP	PL03				28/05/2017	101335	306.00	0.00		Y	306.00		N	
		69	1200	0	Purchase Payment			306.00	0.00	T9		306.00		-	
					306.00 to PI 7	28/05/2017	F-0193					306.00			
70	PP	PL04				28/05/2017	101336	450.00	0.00		Y	450.00		R	31/05/2017
		70	1200	0	Purchase Payment			450.00	0.00	T9		450.00		-	
					450.00 to PI 8	28/05/2017	W/032					450.00			
71	PP	PL01				28/05/2017	BACS	540.00	0.00		Y	540.00		R	31/05/2017
		71	1200	0	Purchase Payment			540.00	0.00	T9		540.00		-	
					540.00 to PI 49	28/05/2017						540.00			
72	BR	1200				14/05/2017	CSH41	220.00	44.00		Y	264.00		R	31/05/2017
		72	4000	0	Staff Member -			220.00	44.00	T1		264.00		N	
73	BR	1200				19/05/2017	Debit Card	45.00	0.00		Y	45.00		R	31/05/2017
		73	4002	0	Jigsaw			45.00	0.00	T0		45.00		N	
74	SP	FF02				17/05/2017	CANCEL	99.60	0.00		N	0.00		R	31/05/2017
		74	1200	0	Cancelled Cheque			99.60	0.00	T9		0.00		-	
75	JC	1200				31/05/2017	CSH25	44.48	0.00		Y	44.48		R	31/05/2017
		75	1200	0	Bank Transfer			44.48	0.00	T9		44.48		-	

Date: 22/08/2017 Time: 20:38:01								Toy Shop Audit Trail (Detailed)						Page: 7
No	**Type**	**A/C**	**N/C**	**Dept**	**Details**	**Date**	**Ref**	**Net**	**Tax**	**T/C**	**Pd**	**Paid**	**V**	**B**	**Bank Rec. Date**
76	JD	1230				31/05/2017	CSH25	44.48	0.00		Y	44.48		-	
		76	1230	0	Bank Transfer			44.48	0.00	T9		44.48		-	
77	JD	1200				31/05/2017	JNL04	10,000.00	0.00		Y	10,000.00		R	31/05/2017
		77	1200	0	Being the proceeds			10,000.00	0.00	T9		10,000.00		-	
78	JC	2300				31/05/2017	JNL04	10,000.00	0.00		Y	10,000.00		-	
		78	2300	0	Being the proceeds			10,000.00	0.00	T9		10,000.00		-	
79	SR	BB01				29/05/2017		3,102.00	0.00		Y	3,102.00		R	31/05/2017
		79	1200	0	Sales Receipt			3,102.00	0.00	T9		3,102.00		-	
					3102.00 to SI 45	29/05/2017	2021					3,102.00			
80	SR	FF02				29/05/2017		400.00	0.00		Y	400.00		R	31/05/2017
		80	1200	0	Sales Receipt			400.00	0.00	T9		400.00		-	
					400.00 to SI 46	29/05/2017	2022					400.00			
81	SR	TP04				29/05/2017		6,000.00	0.00		Y	6,000.00		R	31/05/2017
		81	1200	0	Sales Receipt			6,000.00	0.00	T9		6,000.00		-	
					6000.00 to SI 47	29/05/2017	2023					6,000.00			
82	BP	1200				31/05/2017		101.32	0.00		Y	101.32		R	31/05/2017
		82	7901	0	Charges incurred			101.32	0.00	T2		101.32		N	

(e) Aged Debtors Analysis

Date:	22/08/2017	**Toy Shop**	Page:	1
Time:	20:38:27	**Aged Debtors Analysis (Detailed)**		

Date From:	01/01/1980		Customer From:	
Date To:	22/08/2017		Customer To:	ZZZZZZZZ
Include future transactions:	No			
Exclude later payments:	No			

** NOTE: All report values are shown in Base Currency, unless otherwise indicated **

| A/C: | FF02 | Name: | Forming Fun | | Contact: | | | Tel: | |

No	Type	Date	Ref	Details	Balance	Future	Current	Period 1	Period 2	Period 3	Older
46	SI	04/05/2017	2022	Boxed Games	200.00	0.00	0.00	0.00	0.00	200.00	0.00
74	SP	17/05/2017	CANCEL	Cancelled Cheque	99.60	0.00	0.00	0.00	0.00	99.60	0.00
				Totals:	299.60	0.00	0.00	0.00	0.00	299.60	0.00

Turnover:	599.60
Credit Limit £	4,000.00

| A/C: | SM03 | Name: | Space Models | | Contact: | | | Tel: | |

No	Type	Date	Ref	Details	Balance	Future	Current	Period 1	Period 2	Period 3	Older
3	SI	10/04/2017	093	Opening Balance	1,195.20	0.00	0.00	0.00	0.00	0.00	1,195.20
				Totals:	1,195.20	0.00	0.00	0.00	0.00	0.00	1,195.20

Turnover:	1,195.20
Credit Limit £	3,000.00

| | Grand Totals: | 1,494.80 | 0.00 | 0.00 | 0.00 | 0.00 | 299.60 | 1,195.20 |

(f) Journal Day Book

Date:	22/08/2017		Toy Shop		Page:	1
Time:	20:38:58		Day Books: Nominal Ledger			

Date From:	01/01/1980			N/C From:	
Date To:	31/12/2019			N/C To:	99999999

Transaction From:	1			Dept From:	0
Transaction To:	99,999,999			Dept To:	999

No	Type	N/C	Date	Ref	Ex.Ref	Details	Dept	T/C	Debit	Credit	V	B
9	JD	0040	01/05/2017	O/Bal		Opening Balance	0	T9	5,800.00		-	-
10	JC	9998	01/05/2017	O/Bal		Opening Balance	0	T9		5,800.00	-	-
11	JD	0050	01/05/2017	O/Bal		Opening Balance	0	T9	3,000.00		-	-
12	JC	9998	01/05/2017	O/Bal		Opening Balance	0	T9		3,000.00	-	-
13	JD	1200	01/05/2017	O/Bal		Opening Balance	0	T9	4,225.00		-	-
14	JC	9998	01/05/2017	O/Bal		Opening Balance	0	T9		4,225.00	-	-
15	JD	1230	01/05/2017	O/Bal		Opening Balance	0	T9	300.00		-	-
16	JC	9998	01/05/2017	O/Bal		Opening Balance	0	T9		300.00	-	-
17	JC	2200	01/05/2017	O/Bal		Opening Balance	0	T9		543.00	-	-
18	JD	9998	01/05/2017	O/Bal		Opening Balance	0	T9	543.00		-	-
19	JD	2201	01/05/2017	O/Bal		Opening Balance	0	T9	109.00		-	-
20	JC	9998	01/05/2017	O/Bal		Opening Balance	0	T9		109.00	-	-
21	JC	3000	01/05/2017	O/Bal		Opening Balance	0	T9		20,000.00	-	-
22	JD	9998	01/05/2017	O/Bal		Opening Balance	0	T9	20,000.00		-	-
23	JD	3260	01/05/2017	O/Bal		Opening Balance	0	T9	355.00		-	-
24	JC	9998	01/05/2017	O/Bal		Opening Balance	0	T9		355.00	-	-
25	JC	4000	01/05/2017	O/Bal		Opening Balance	0	T9		6,080.00	-	-
26	JD	9998	01/05/2017	O/Bal		Opening Balance	0	T9	6,080.00		-	-
27	JC	4002	01/05/2017	O/Bal		Opening Balance	0	T9		700.00	-	-
28	JD	9998	01/05/2017	O/Bal		Opening Balance	0	T9	700.00		-	-
29	JC	4001	01/05/2017	O/Bal		Opening Balance	0	T9		1,967.00	-	-
30	JD	9998	01/05/2017	O/Bal		Opening Balance	0	T9	1,967.00		-	-
31	JD	5000	01/05/2017	O/Bal		Opening Balance	0	T9	8,000.00		-	-
32	JC	9998	01/05/2017	O/Bal		Opening Balance	0	T9		8,000.00	-	-
33	JD	5002	01/05/2017	O/Bal		Opening Balance	0	T9	3,200.00		-	-
34	JC	9998	01/05/2017	O/Bal		Opening Balance	0	T9		3,200.00	-	-
35	JD	5001	01/05/2017	O/Bal		Opening Balance	0	T9	2,465.00		-	-
36	JC	9998	01/05/2017	O/Bal		Opening Balance	0	T9		2,465.00	-	-
37	JD	7504	01/05/2017	O/Bal		Opening Balance	0	T9	53.00		-	-
38	JC	9998	01/05/2017	O/Bal		Opening Balance	0	T9		53.00	-	-
39	JD	7200	01/05/2017	O/Bal		Opening Balance	0	T9	167.00		-	-
40	JC	9998	01/05/2017	O/Bal		Opening Balance	0	T9		167.00	-	-
41	JD	7100	01/05/2017	O/Bal		Opening Balance	0	T9	1,550.00		-	-
42	JC	9998	01/05/2017	O/Bal		Opening Balance	0	T9		1,550.00	-	-
43	JC	1200	01/05/2017	TRANS01		Bank Transfer	0	T9		500.00	-	R
44	JD	1210	01/05/2017	TRANS01		Bank Transfer	0	T9	500.00		-	N
65	JD	3260	25/05/2017	JNL02		Transfer of cash for James	0	T9	2,000.00		-	-
66	JC	1200	25/05/2017	JNL02		James Free's personal use	0	T9		2,000.00	-	R
67	JD	7201	31/05/2017	JNL03		Being the transfer of gas	0	T9	502.00		-	-
68	JC	7100	31/05/2017	JNL03		Being the transfer of gas	0	T9		502.00	-	-
75	JC	1200	31/05/2017	CSH25		Bank Transfer	0	T9		44.48	-	R
76	JD	1230	31/05/2017	CSH25		Bank Transfer	0	T9	44.48		-	-
77	JD	1200	31/05/2017	JNL04		Being the proceeds received	0	T9	10,000.00		-	R
78	JC	2300	31/05/2017	JNL04		Being the proceeds received	0	T9		10,000.00	-	-
								Totals:	71,560.48	71,560.48		

(g) Bank Reconciliation Report

Date:	22/08/2017					**Toy Shop**			**Page:**	1
Time:	20:39:30					**Bank Reconciled Transactions**				

Bank Reconciled On: 31/05/2017

No	Type	Date	A/C	N/C	Dept	Ref	Details	Net	Tax	T/C
13	JD	01/05/2017	1200	1200	0	O/Bal	Opening Balance	4,225.00	0.00	T9
43	JC	01/05/2017	1200	1200	0	TRANS01	Bank Transfer	500.00	0.00	T9
54	BR	13/05/2017	1200	4000	0	Cash Sales	Computer Games	1,000.00	200.00	T1
55	BR	13/05/2017	1200	4001	0	Cash Sales	Boxed Games	2,399.50	479.90	T1
56	BR	20/05/2017	1200	4000	0	Cash Sales	Computer Games	995.00	0.00	T0
57	SR	17/05/2017	BB01	1200	0		Sales Receipt	349.20	0.00	T9
58	SR	17/05/2017	FF02	1200	0	CANCEL	Sales Receipt	99.60	0.00	T9
59	SR	26/05/2017	TP04	1200	0		Sales Receipt	195.60	0.00	T9
60	PP	22/05/2017	PL01	1200	0	101333	Purchase Payment	369.60	0.00	T9
61	PP	22/05/2017	PL02	1200	0	101334	Purchase Payment	1,005.60	0.00	T9
62	BP	31/05/2017	1200	7104	0	DD/STO	Galloway Union	100.00	0.00	T9
66	JC	25/05/2017	1200	1200	0	JNL02	James Free's personal use	2,000.00	0.00	T9
70	PP	28/05/2017	PL04	1200	0	101336	Purchase Payment	450.00	0.00	T9
71	PP	28/05/2017	PL01	1200	0	BACS	Purchase Payment	540.00	0.00	T9
72	BR	14/05/2017	1200	4000	0	CSH41	Staff Member - Computer	220.00	44.00	T1
73	BR	19/05/2017	1200	4002	0	Debit Card	Jigsaw	45.00	0.00	T0
74	SP	17/05/2017	FF02	1200	0	CANCEL	Cancelled Cheque	99.60	0.00	T9
75	JC	31/05/2017	1200	1200	0	CSH25	Bank Transfer	44.48	0.00	T9
77	JD	31/05/2017	1200	1200	0	JNL04	Being the proceeds received	10,000.00	0.00	T9
79	SR	29/05/2017	BB01	1200	0		Sales Receipt	3,102.00	0.00	T9
80	SR	29/05/2017	FF02	1200	0		Sales Receipt	400.00	0.00	T9
81	SR	29/05/2017	TP04	1200	0		Sales Receipt	6,000.00	0.00	T9
82	BP	31/05/2017	1200	7901	0		Charges incurred	101.32	0.00	T2

PRACTICE PAPER 2

CRAZY HAIR ANSWERS

TASK 3.3

(a) Customer Address List

Date: 22/08/2017	**Crazy Hair**		**Page:** 1	
Time: 21:18:50	**Customer Address List**			

Customer From:
Customer To: ZZZZZZZZ

A/C	Name & Address	Contact Name	Telephone	Fax
104	Alfred Images Masuki Offices PO Box 5684 Birmingham B23 4RD			
110	Figgaro Beta Studio 34 Knightsbridge Way Morden SE23 4KA			
118	Blades Alpha Studio 45 Key West London SE1 0JF			
122	Hair Studio Framlington Court Lee London SE4 7YH			
138	Ribbons and Curls PO Box 1120 Canning Town London TN2 2EB			

(b) Supplier Address List

Date: 22/08/2017		**Crazy Hair**		**Page:** 1
Time: 21:19:28		**Supplier Address List**		

Supplier From:
Supplier To: ZZZZZZZZ

A/C	Name	Contact	Telephone	Fax
1134	Avada Cash & Carry 32 Surrey Quay Isle of Dogs E12 3NW			
1138	Straightside Supplies Havering Place Holborn London WC1 2PP			
1165	Hair Supplies 43 St Helens Way London SE7 3RF			
1185	Wig Specialists Retro Square 32 Wigmore Road London EC1V 3SG			

(c) Trial Balance

Date: 22/08/2017		**Crazy Hair**		**Page:** 1
Time: 21:19:56		**Period Trial Balance**		

To Period: Month 12, February 2018

N/C	Name	Debit	Credit
0040	Furniture and Fixtures	31,000.00	
0050	Motor Vehicles	24,000.00	
1100	Debtors Control Account	8,907.60	
1200	Bank Current Account	54,210.81	
1230	Petty Cash	200.00	
2100	Creditors Control Account		7,214.40
2200	Sales Tax Control Account		5,550.00
2201	Purchase Tax Control Account	1,507.94	
3000	Capital		165,000.00
3260	Drawings	5,000.00	
4000	Sales – Brushes		345.00
4001	Sales – Combs		187.00
4002	Sales – Colours		3,801.45
4003	Sales – Hairdryers		758.00
4004	Sales – Wigs		5,600.00
4005	Cash Sales		617.50
5000	Purchases – Brushes	873.00	
5001	Purchases – Combs	50.00	
5002	Purchases – Colours	4,200.00	
5003	Purchases – Hairdryers	6,310.00	
5004	Purchases – Wigs	52,814.00	
	Totals:	**189,073.35**	**189,073.35**

TASK 9

Screen shot to show setting up the recurring entry

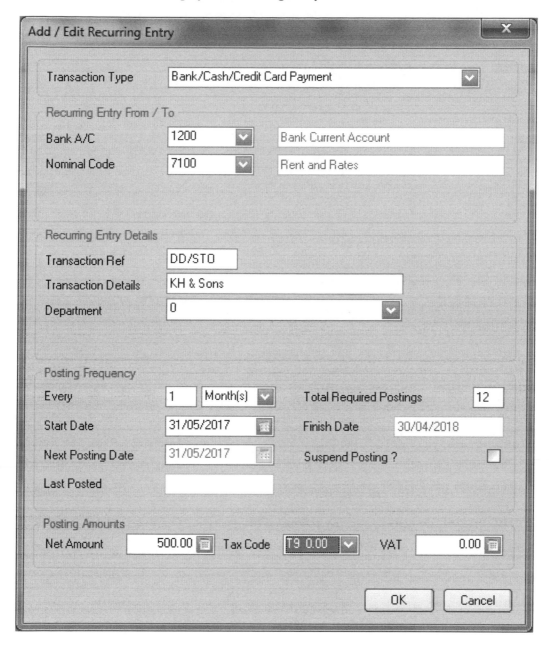

TASK 12

Screen shot to show change of customer address

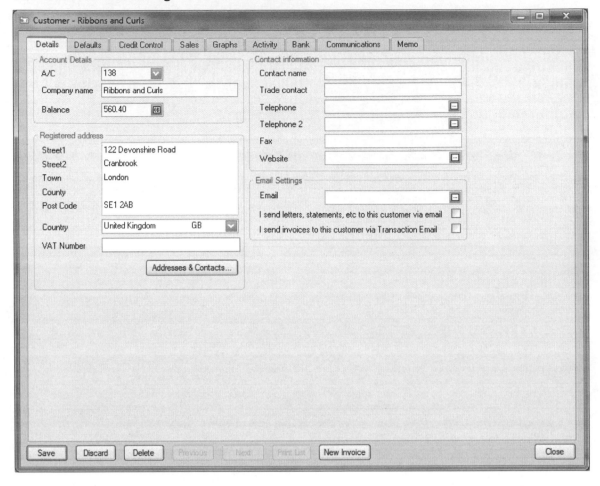

TASK 16

(a) Customer Address list

Date:	22/08/2017	**Crazy Hair**		**Page:** 1
Time:	21:50:40	**Customer Address List**		

Customer From:
Customer To: ZZZZZZZZ

A/C	Name & Address	Contact Name	Telephone	Fax
104	Alfred Images Masuki Offices PO Box 5684 Birmingham B23 4RD			
110	Figgaro Beta Studio 34 Knightsbridge Way Morden SE23 4KA			
118	Blades Alpha Studio 45 Key West London SE1 0JF			
122	Hair Studio Framlington Court Lee London SE4 7YH			
138	Ribbons and Curls 122 Devonshire Road Cranbrook London SE1 2AB			

(b) Sales Day Book

Date:	22/08/2017	**Crazy Hair**		**Page:** 1
Time:	21:55:42	**Day Books: Customer Invoices (Detailed)**		

Date From:	01/01/1980		**Customer From:**	
Date To:	31/12/2019		**Customer To:**	ZZZZZZZZ
Transaction From:	1		**N/C From:**	
Transaction To:	99,999,999		**N/C To:**	99999999
Dept From:	0			
Dept To:	999			

Tran No.	Type	Date	A/C Ref	N/C	Inv Ref	Dept.	Details	Net Amount	Tax Amount	T/C	Gross Amount	V	B
1	SI	02/04/2017	104	9998	3352	0	Opening Balance	1,809.60	0.00	T9	1,809.60	-	-
2	SI	10/04/2017	110	9998	2856	0	Opening Balance	3,880.80	0.00	T9	3,880.80	-	-
3	SI	18/04/2017	118	9998	3345	0	Opening Balance	2,144.40	0.00	T9	2,144.40	-	-
4	SI	12/04/2017	122	9998	3098	0	Opening Balance	681.60	0.00	T9	681.60	-	-
5	SI	12/04/2017	138	9998	3123	0	Opening Balance	391.20	0.00	T9	391.20	-	-
48	SI	12/05/2017	138	4002	3353	0	10 x Colours	141.00	28.20	T1	169.20	N	-
49	SI	12/05/2017	104	4000	3354	0	50 x Brushes	581.00	116.20	T1	697.20	N	-
50	SI	13/05/2017	110	4003	3355	0	12 x Hairdryers	660.00	132.00	T1	792.00	N	-
51	SI	15/05/2017	118	4004	3356	0	8 x Wigs	1,685.76	337.15	T1	2,022.91	N	-
52	SI	15/05/2017	118	4003	3356	0	3 x Hairdryers	203.40	40.68	T1	244.08	N	-
53	SI	18/05/2017	122	4000	3357	0	12 x Brushes	316.80	63.36	T1	380.16	N	-
54	SI	18/05/2017	122	4004	3357	0	4 x Wigs	881.92	176.38	T1	1,058.30	N	-
55	SI	18/05/2017	122	4002	3357	0	16 x Colours	230.40	46.08	T1	276.48	N	-
							Totals:	13,607.88	940.05		14,547.93		

(c) Sales Returns Day Book

Date:	22/08/2017			**Crazy Hair**					Page:	1
Time:	21:56:07			**Day Books: Customer Credits (Detailed)**						

Date From:	01/01/1980						Customer From:		
Date To:	31/12/2019						Customer To:	ZZZZZZZZZ	
Transaction From:	1						N/C From:		
Transaction To:	99,999,999						N/C To:	99999999	
Dept From:	0								
Dept To:	999								

Tran No.	Type	Date	A/C Ref	N/C	Inv Ref	Dept.	Details	Net Amount	Tax Amount	T/C	Gross Amount	V	B
56	SC	25/05/2017	104	4000	CN23	0	Return of Brushes	56.00	11.20	T1	67.20	N	-
							Totals:	56.00	11.20		67.20		

(d) Purchases Day Book

Date:	22/08/2017			**Crazy Hair**					Page:	1
Time:	21:56:48			**Day Books: Supplier Invoices (Detailed)**						

Date From:	01/01/1980						Supplier From:		
Date To:	31/12/2019						Supplier To:	ZZZZZZZZZ	
Transaction From:	1						N/C From:		
Transaction To:	99,999,999						N/C To:	99999999	
Dept From:	0								
Dept To:	999								

Tran No.	Type	Date	A/C Ref	N/C	Inv Ref	Dept	Details	Net Amount	Tax Amount	T/C	Gross Amount	V	B
6	PI	22/04/2017	1134	9998	C/251	0	Opening Balance	4,454.40	0.00	T9	4,454.40	-	-
7	PI	11/04/2017	1138	9998	9140	0	Opening Balance	1,839.60	0.00	T9	1,839.60	-	-
8	PI	11/04/2017	1165	9998	0028	0	Opening Balance	818.40	0.00	T9	818.40	-	-
9	PI	18/04/2017	1185	9998	S653	0	Opening Balance	102.00	0.00	T9	102.00	-	-
57	PI	11/05/2017	1138	5000		0	Brushes	191.60	38.32	T1	229.92	N	-
58	PI	11/05/2017	1134	5002		0	Colours	954.00	190.80	T1	1,144.80	N	-
59	PI	13/05/2017	1165	5003		0	Hairdryers	178.56	0.00	T0	178.56	N	-
60	PI	14/05/2017	1185	5004		0	Wigs	3,393.60	678.72	T1	4,072.32	N	-
							Totals	11,932.16	907.84		12,840.00		

(e) Customer Activity (detailed report)

Date: 22/08/2017	**Time:** 21:51:03

Crazy Hair

Customer Activity (Detailed)

Page: 1

Date From:	01/01/1980	Customer From:	
Date To:	31/05/2017	Customer To:	ZZZZZZZZ
Transaction From:	1	N/C From:	
Transaction To:	99,999,999	N/C To:	99999999
Inc b/fwd transaction:	No	Dept From:	0
Exc later payment:	No	Dept To:	999

** NOTE: All report values are shown in Base Currency, unless otherwise indicated **

A/C: 104   Name: Alfred Images   Contact: Tel:

No	Type	Date	Ref	N/C	Details	Dept	T/C	Value	O/S	Debit	Credit	V	B
1	SI	02/04/2017	3352	9998	Opening Balance	0	T9	1,809.60		1,809.60		-	-
49	SI	12/05/2017	3354	4000	50 x Brushes	0	T1	697.20 *	697.20	697.20		N	-
56	SC	25/05/2017	CN23	4000	Return of Brushes	0	T1	67.20 *	-67.20		67.20	N	-
63	SR	20/05/2017	183001	1200	Sales Receipt	0	T9	1,809.60			1,809.60	-	R
					Totals:			630.00	630.00	2,506.80	1,876.80		

Amount Outstanding	630.00
Amount Paid this period	1,809.60
Credit Limit £	8,000.00
Turnover YTD	2,334.60

A/C: 110   Name: Figgaro   Contact: Tel:

No	Type	Date	Ref	N/C	Details	Dept	T/C	Value	O/S	Debit	Credit	V	B
2	SI	10/04/2017	2856	9998	Opening Balance	0	T9	3,880.80		3,880.80		-	-
50	SI	13/05/2017	3355	4003	12 x Hairdryers	0	T1	792.00 *	792.00	792.00		N	-
65	SR	21/05/2017	BACS	1200	Sales Receipt	0	T9	3,880.80			3,880.80	-	R
					Totals:			792.00	792.00	4,672.80	3,880.80		

Amount Outstanding	792.00
Amount Paid this period	3,880.80
Credit Limit £	6,500.00
Turnover YTD	4,540.80

A/C: 118   Name: Blades   Contact: Tel:

No	Type	Date	Ref	N/C	Details	Dept	T/C	Value	O/S	Debit	Credit	V	B
3	SI	18/04/2017	3345	9998	Opening Balance	0	T9	2,144.40		2,144.40		-	-
51	SI	15/05/2017	3356	4004	8 x Wigs	0	T1	2,022.91 *	2,022.91	2,022.91		N	-
52	SI	15/05/2017	3356	4003	3 x Hairdryers	0	T1	244.08 *	244.08	244.08		N	-
64	SR	21/05/2017	654255	1200	Sales Receipt	0	T9	2,144.40			2,144.40	-	R
					Totals:			2,266.99	2,266.99	4,411.39	2,144.40		

Amount Outstanding	2,266.99
Amount Paid this period	2,144.40
Credit Limit £	6,100.00
Turnover YTD	4,033.56

A/C: 122   Name: Hair Studio   Contact: Tel:

No	Type	Date	Ref	N/C	Details	Dept	T/C	Value	O/S	Debit	Credit	V	B
4	SI	12/04/2017	3098	9998	Opening Balance	0	T9	681.60		681.60		-	-
53	SI	18/05/2017	3357	4000	12 x Brushes	0	T1	380.16 *	380.16	380.16		N	-
54	SI	18/05/2017	3357	4004	4 x Wigs	0	T1	1,058.30 *	1,058.30	1,058.30		N	-
55	SI	18/05/2017	3357	4002	16 x Colours	0	T1	276.48 *	276.48	276.48		N	-
66	SR	21/05/2017	CANCEL	1200	Sales Receipt	0	T9	681.60			681.60	-	R
75	SP	21/05/2017	CANCEL	1200	Cancelled Cheque	0	T9	681.60	681.60	681.60		-	R
					Totals:			2,396.54	2,396.54	3,078.14	681.60		

Amount Outstanding	2,396.54
Amount Paid this period	0.00
Credit Limit £	5,000.00
Turnover YTD	2,110.72

| Date: | 22/08/2017 | **Crazy Hair** | Page: | 2 |
| Time: | 21:51:03 | **Customer Activity (Detailed)** | | |

| A/C: | 138 | Name: | Ribbons and Curls | | Contact: | | | Tel: | | |

No	Type	Date	Ref	N/C	Details	Dept	T/C	Value	O/S	Debit	Credit	V	B
5	SI	12/04/2017	3123	9998	Opening Balance	0	T9	391.20 *	391.20	391.20		-	-
48	SI	12/05/2017	3353	4002	10 x Colours	0	T1	169.20 *	169.20	169.20		N	-
					Totals:			560.40	560.40	560.40			

Amount Outstanding	560.40
Amount Paid this period	0.00
Credit Limit £	5,000.00
Turnover YTD	532.20

(f) Supplier Activity (detailed report)

| Date: | 22/08/2017 | **Crazy Hair** | Page: | 1 |
| Time: | 21:51:30 | **Supplier Activity (Detailed)** | | |

Date From:	01/01/1980		Supplier From:	
Date To:	31/05/2017		Supplier To:	ZZZZZZZZ
Transaction From:	1		N/C From:	
Transaction To:	99,999,999		N/C To:	99999999
Inc b/fwd transaction:	No		Dept From:	0
Exc later payment:	No		Dept To:	999

** NOTE: All report values are shown in Base Currency, unless otherwise indicated **

| A/C: | 1134 | Name: | Avada Cash & Carry | | Contact: | | | Tel: | | |

No	Type	Date	Ref	N/C	Details	Dept	T/C	Value	O/S	Debit	Credit	V	B
6	PI	22/04/2017	C/251	9998	Opening Balance	0	T9	4,454.40	0.00		4,454.40	-	-
58	PI	11/05/2017		5002	Colours	0	T1	1,144.80 *	1,144.80		1,144.80	N	-
68	PP	31/05/2017	163456	1200	Purchase Payment	0	T9	4,454.40	0.00	4,454.40		-	N
					Totals:			1,144.80	1,144.80	4,454.40	5,599.20		

Amount Outstanding	1,144.80
Amount paid this period	4,454.40
Credit Limit £	5,500.00
Turnover YTD	5,408.40

| A/C: | 1138 | Name: | Straightside Supplies | | Contact: | | | Tel: | | |

No	Type	Date	Ref	N/C	Details	Dept	T/C	Value	O/S	Debit	Credit	V	B
7	PI	11/04/2017	9140	9998	Opening Balance	0	T9	1,839.60 *	1,839.60		1,839.60	-	-
57	PI	11/05/2017		5000	Brushes	0	T1	229.92 *	229.92		229.92	N	-
					Totals:			2,069.52	2,069.52	0.00	2,069.52		

Amount Outstanding	2,069.52
Amount paid this period	0.00
Credit Limit £	12,000.00
Turnover YTD	2,031.20

| A/C: | 1165 | Name: | Hair Supplies | | Contact: | | | Tel: | | |

No	Type	Date	Ref	N/C	Details	Dept	T/C	Value	O/S	Debit	Credit	V	B
8	PI	11/04/2017	0028	9998	Opening Balance	0	T9	818.40	0.00		818.40	-	-
59	PI	13/05/2017		5003	Hairdryers	0	T0	178.56 *	178.56		178.56	N	-
69	PP	31/05/2017	163457	1200	Purchase Payment	0	T9	818.40	0.00	818.40		-	N
					Totals:			178.56	178.56	818.40	996.96		

Amount Outstanding	178.56
Amount paid this period	818.40
Credit Limit £	4,000.00
Turnover YTD	996.96

| A/C: | 1185 | Name: | Wig Specialists | | Contact: | | | Tel: | | |

No	Type	Date	Ref	N/C	Details	Dept	T/C	Value	O/S	Debit	Credit	V	B
9	PI	18/04/2017	S653	9998	Opening Balance	0	T9	102.00	0.00		102.00	-	-
60	PI	14/05/2017		5004	Wigs	0	T1	4,072.32 *	4,072.32		4,072.32	N	-
61	PC	18/05/2017		5004	Wigs	0	T1	123.24 *	-123.24	123.24		N	-
67	PP	31/05/2017	163455	1200	Purchase Payment	0	T9	102.00	0.00	102.00		-	N
					Totals:			3,949.08	3,949.08	225.24	4,174.32		

Amount Outstanding	3,949.08
Amount paid this period	102.00
Credit Limit £	5,000.00
Turnover YTD	3,392.90

(g) Period Trial Balance for the end of May

Date:	22/08/2017	**Crazy Hair**	Page:	1
Time:	21:52:08	**Period Trial Balance**		

To Period: Month 3, May 2017

N/C	Name	Debit	Credit
0040	Furniture and Fixtures	31,000.00	
0050	Motor Vehicles	24,000.00	
1100	Debtors Control Account	6,645.93	
1200	Bank Current Account	55,459.24	
1230	Petty Cash	185.69	
2100	Creditors Control Account		7,341.96
2200	Sales Tax Control Account		6,482.35
2201	Purchase Tax Control Account	2,401.96	
3000	Capital		165,000.00
3260	Drawings	5,440.00	
4000	Sales - Brushes		1,204.30
4001	Sales - Combs		187.00
4002	Sales - Colours		4,172.85
4003	Sales - Hairdryers		1,621.40
4004	Sales - Wigs		8,167.68
4005	Cash Sales		617.50
5000	Purchases - Brushes	1,064.60	
5001	Purchases - Combs	50.00	
5002	Purchases - Colours	5,154.00	
5003	Purchases - Hairdryers	6,488.56	
5004	Purchases - Wigs	56,104.90	
7100	Rent and Rates	500.00	
7104	Premises Insurance	168.00	
7200	Electricity	66.94	
7400	Travelling	33.60	
7501	Postage and Carriage	4.51	
7901	Bank Charges	27.11	
	Totals:	194,795.04	194,795.04

(h) Audit Trail for May

Date:	22/08/2017	**Crazy Hair**			Page:	1
Time:	21:52:57	**Audit Trail (Summary)**				

Date From:	01/05/2017		Customer From:	
Date To:	31/05/2017		Customer To:	ZZZZZZZZ
Transaction From:	1		Supplier From:	
Transaction To:	99,999,999		Supplier To:	ZZZZZZZZ
Dept From:	0		N/C From:	
Dept To:	999		N/C To:	99999999
Exclude Deleted Tran:	No			

No	Type	Date	A/C	N/C	Dept	Ref	Details	Net	Tax	T/C	Pd	Paid	V	B	Bank Rec. Date
10	JD	01/05/2017	0050	0050	0	O/Bal	Opening Balance	24,000.00	0.00	T9	Y	24,000.00	-	-	
11	JC	01/05/2017	9998	9998	0	O/Bal	Opening Balance	24,000.00	0.00	T9	Y	24,000.00	-	-	
12	JD	01/05/2017	0040	0040	0	O/Bal	Opening Balance	31,000.00	0.00	T9	Y	31,000.00	-	-	
13	JC	01/05/2017	9998	9998	0	O/Bal	Opening Balance	31,000.00	0.00	T9	Y	31,000.00	-	-	
14	JD	01/05/2017	1200	1200	0	O/Bal	Opening Balance	54,210.81	0.00	T9	Y	54,210.81	-	-	31/05/2017
15	JC	01/05/2017	9998	9998	0	O/Bal	Opening Balance	54,210.81	0.00	T9	Y	54,210.81	-	-	
16	JD	01/05/2017	1230	1230	0	O/Bal	Opening Balance	200.00	0.00	T9	Y	200.00	-	-	31/05/2017
17	JC	01/05/2017	9998	9998	0	O/Bal	Opening Balance	200.00	0.00	T9	Y	200.00	-	-	
18	JC	01/05/2017	2200	2200	0	O/Bal	Opening Balance	5,550.00	0.00	T9	Y	5,550.00	-	-	
19	JD	01/05/2017	9998	9998	0	O/Bal	Opening Balance	5,550.00	0.00	T9	Y	5,550.00	-	-	
20	JD	01/05/2017	2201	2201	0	O/Bal	Opening Balance	1,507.94	0.00	T9	Y	1,507.94	-	-	
21	JC	01/05/2017	9998	9998	0	O/Bal	Opening Balance	1,507.94	0.00	T9	Y	1,507.94	-	-	
22	JC	01/05/2017	3000	3000	0	O/Bal	Opening Balance	165,000.00	0.00	T9	Y	165,000.00	-	-	
23	JD	01/05/2017	9998	9998	0	O/Bal	Opening Balance	165,000.00	0.00	T9	Y	165,000.00	-	-	
24	JD	01/05/2017	3260	3260	0	O/Bal	Opening Balance	5,000.00	0.00	T9	Y	5,000.00	-	-	
25	JC	01/05/2017	9998	9998	0	O/Bal	Opening Balance	5,000.00	0.00	T9	Y	5,000.00	-	-	
26	JC	01/05/2017	4000	4000	0	O/Bal	Opening Balance	345.00	0.00	T9	Y	345.00	-	-	
27	JD	01/05/2017	9998	9998	0	O/Bal	Opening Balance	345.00	0.00	T9	Y	345.00	-	-	
28	JC	01/05/2017	4001	4001	0	O/Bal	Opening Balance	187.00	0.00	T9	Y	187.00	-	-	
29	JD	01/05/2017	9998	9998	0	O/Bal	Opening Balance	187.00	0.00	T9	Y	187.00	-	-	
30	JC	01/05/2017	4002	4002	0	O/Bal	Opening Balance	3,801.45	0.00	T9	Y	3,801.45	-	-	
31	JD	01/05/2017	9998	9998	0	O/Bal	Opening Balance	3,801.45	0.00	T9	Y	3,801.45	-	-	
32	JC	01/05/2017	4003	4003	0	O/Bal	Opening Balance	758.00	0.00	T9	Y	758.00	-	-	
33	JD	01/05/2017	9998	9998	0	O/Bal	Opening Balance	758.00	0.00	T9	Y	758.00	-	-	
34	JC	01/05/2017	4004	4004	0	O/Bal	Opening Balance	5,600.00	0.00	T9	Y	5,600.00	-	-	
35	JD	01/05/2017	9998	9998	0	O/Bal	Opening Balance	5,600.00	0.00	T9	Y	5,600.00	-	-	
36	JC	01/05/2017	4005	4005	0	O/Bal	Opening Balance	617.50	0.00	T9	Y	617.50	-	-	
37	JD	01/05/2017	9998	9998	0	O/Bal	Opening Balance	617.50	0.00	T9	Y	617.50	-	-	
38	JD	01/05/2017	5000	5000	0	O/Bal	Opening Balance	873.00	0.00	T9	Y	873.00	-	-	
39	JC	01/05/2017	9998	9998	0	O/Bal	Opening Balance	873.00	0.00	T9	Y	873.00	-	-	

Date:	22/08/2017	**Crazy Hair**			Page:	2
Time:	21:52:57	**Audit Trail (Summary)**				

No	Type	Date	A/C	N/C	Dept	Ref	Details	Net	Tax	T/C	Pd	Paid	V	B	Bank Rec. Date
40	JD	01/05/2017	5001	5001	0	O/Bal	Opening Balance	50.00	0.00	T9	Y	50.00	-	-	
41	JC	01/05/2017	9998	9998	0	O/Bal	Opening Balance	50.00	0.00	T9	Y	50.00	-	-	
42	JD	01/05/2017	5002	5002	0	O/Bal	Opening Balance	4,200.00	0.00	T9	Y	4,200.00	-	-	
43	JC	01/05/2017	9998	9998	0	O/Bal	Opening Balance	4,200.00	0.00	T9	Y	4,200.00	-	-	
44	JD	01/05/2017	5003	5003	0	O/Bal	Opening Balance	6,310.00	0.00	T9	Y	6,310.00	-	-	
45	JC	01/05/2017	9998	9998	0	O/Bal	Opening Balance	6,310.00	0.00	T9	Y	6,310.00	-	-	
46	JD	01/05/2017	5004	5004	0	O/Bal	Opening Balance	52,814.00	0.00	T9	Y	52,814.00	-	-	
47	JC	01/05/2017	9998	9998	0	O/Bal	Opening Balance	52,814.00	0.00	T9	Y	52,814.00	-	-	
48	SI	12/05/2017	138	4002	0	3353	10 x Colours	141.00	28.20	T1	N	0.00	N	-	
49	SI	12/05/2017	104	4000	0	3354	50 x Brushes	581.00	116.20	T1	N	0.00	N	-	
50	SI	13/05/2017	110	4003	0	3355	12 x Hairdryers	660.00	132.00	T1	N	0.00	N	-	
51	SI	15/05/2017	118	4004	0	3356	8 x Wigs	1,685.76	337.15	T1	N	0.00	N	-	
52	SI	15/05/2017	118	4003	0	3356	3 x Hairdryers	203.40	40.68	T1	N	0.00	N	-	
53	SI	18/05/2017	122	4000	0	3357	12 x Brushes	316.80	63.36	T1	N	0.00	N	-	
54	SI	18/05/2017	122	4004	0	3357	4 x Wigs	881.92	176.38	T1	N	0.00	N	-	
55	SI	18/05/2017	122	4002	0	3357	16 x Colours	230.40	46.08	T1	N	0.00	N	-	
56	SC	25/05/2017	104	4000	0	CN23	Return of Brushes	56.00	11.20	T1	N	0.00	N	-	
57	PI	11/05/2017	1138	5000	0		Brushes	191.60	38.32	T1	N	0.00	N	-	
58	PI	11/05/2017	1134	5002	0		Colours	954.00	190.80	T1	N	0.00	N	-	
59	PI	13/05/2017	1165	5003	0		Hairdryers	178.56	0.00	T0	N	0.00	N	-	
60	PI	14/05/2017	1185	5004	0		Wigs	3,393.60	678.72	T1	N	0.00	N	-	
61	PC	18/05/2017	1185	5004	0		Wigs	102.70	20.54	T1	N	0.00	N	-	
62	BR	20/05/2017	1200	4000	0	1001	Staff Purchase - Brush	17.50	3.50	T1	Y	21.00	N	R	31/05/2017
63	SR	20/05/2017	104	1200	0	183001	Sales Receipt	1,809.60	0.00	T9	Y	1,809.60	-	R	31/05/2017
64	SR	21/05/2017	118	1200	0	654255	Sales Receipt	2,144.40	0.00	T9	Y	2,144.40	-	R	31/05/2017
65	SR	21/05/2017	110	1200	0	BACS	Sales Receipt	3,880.80	0.00	T9	Y	3,880.80	-	R	31/05/2017
66	SR	21/05/2017	122	1200	0	CANCEL	Sales Receipt	681.60	0.00	T9	Y	681.60	-	R	31/05/2017
67	PP	31/05/2017	1185	1200	0	163455	Purchase Payment	102.00	0.00	T9	Y	102.00	-	N	
68	PP	31/05/2017	1134	1200	0	163456	Purchase Payment	4,454.40	0.00	T9	Y	4,454.40	-	N	
69	PP	31/05/2017	1165	1200	0	163457	Purchase Payment	818.40	0.00	T9	Y	818.40	-	N	
70	BP	31/05/2017	1200	7100	0	DD/STO	KH & Sons	500.00	0.00	T9	Y	500.00	-	R	31/05/2017
71	CP	19/05/2017	1230	7400	0	CSH 86	Petty Cash	33.60	6.72	T1	Y	40.32	N	-	
72	CP	20/05/2017	1230	7501	0	CSH 87	Petty Cash	4.51	0.00	T9	Y	4.51	-	-	
73	JD	24/05/2017	3260	3260	0	JH12	Being the transfer of cash for personal use	440.00	0.00	T9	Y	440.00	-	-	
74	JC	24/05/2017	1200	1200	0	JH12	Being the transfer of cash for personal use	440.00	0.00	T9	Y	440.00	-	R	31/05/2017
75	SP	21/05/2017	122	1200	0	CANCEL	Cancelled Cheque	681.60	0.00	T9	N	0.00	-	R	31/05/2017
76	JC	31/05/2017	1200	1200	0	TRF01	Bank Transfer	30.52	0.00	T9	Y	30.52	-	R	31/05/2017
77	JD	31/05/2017	1230	1230	0	TRF01	Bank Transfer	30.52	0.00	T9	Y	30.52	-	-	
78	BP	24/05/2017	1200	7104	0	DD	Coopers Union	168.00	0.00	T9	Y	168.00	-	R	31/05/2017

Date:	22/08/2017	**Crazy Hair**			Page:	3
Time:	21:52:57	**Audit Trail (Summary)**				

No	Type	Date	A/C	N/C	Dept	Ref	Details	Net	Tax	T/C	Pd	Paid	V	B	Bank Rec. Date
79	BP	31/05/2017	1200	7200	0	DD	Electricity	66.94	0.00	T9	Y	66.94	-	R	31/05/2017
80	BP	31/05/2017	1200	7901	0		Charges incurred	27.11	0.00	T2	Y	27.11	N	R	31/05/2017

(i) Aged Creditors

| Date: | 22/08/2017 | **Crazy Hair** | | Page: | 1 |
| Time: | 21:53:24 | **Aged Creditors Analysis (Detailed)** | | | |

| Date From: | 01/01/1980 | | Supplier From: | |
| Date To: | 31/05/2017 | | Supplier To: | ZZZZZZZZ |

Include future transactions: No
Exclude later payments: No

** NOTE: All report values are shown in Base Currency, unless otherwise indicated **

| A/C: | 1134 | Name: | Avada Cash & Carry | | Contact: | | | | Tel: | | |

No:	Type	Date	Ref	Details	Balance	Future	Current	Period 1	Period 2	Period 3	Older
58	PI	11/05/2017		Colours	1,144.80	0.00	1,144.80	0.00	0.00	0.00	0.00
				Totals:	1,144.80	0.00	1,144.80	0.00	0.00	0.00	0.00

Turnover: 5,408.40
Credit Limit £ 5,500.00

| A/C: | 1138 | Name: | Straightside Supplies | | Contact: | | | | Tel: | | |

No:	Type	Date	Ref	Details	Balance	Future	Current	Period 1	Period 2	Period 3	Older
7	PI	11/04/2017	9140	Opening Balance	1,839.60	0.00	0.00	1,839.60	0.00	0.00	0.00
57	PI	11/05/2017		Brushes	229.92	0.00	229.92	0.00	0.00	0.00	0.00
				Totals:	2,069.52	0.00	229.92	1,839.60	0.00	0.00	0.00

Turnover: 2,031.20
Credit Limit £ 12,000.00

| A/C: | 1165 | Name: | Hair Supplies | | Contact: | | | | Tel: | | |

No:	Type	Date	Ref	Details	Balance	Future	Current	Period 1	Period 2	Period 3	Older
59	PI	13/05/2017		Hairdryers	178.56	0.00	178.56	0.00	0.00	0.00	0.00
				Totals:	178.56	0.00	178.56	0.00	0.00	0.00	0.00

Turnover: 996.96
Credit Limit £ 4,000.00

| A/C: | 1185 | Name: | Wig Specialists | | Contact: | | | | Tel: | | |

No:	Type	Date	Ref	Details	Balance	Future	Current	Period 1	Period 2	Period 3	Older
60	PI	14/05/2017		Wigs	4,072.32	0.00	4,072.32	0.00	0.00	0.00	0.00
61	PC	18/05/2017		Wigs	-123.24	0.00	-123.24	0.00	0.00	0.00	0.00
				Totals:	3,949.08	0.00	3,949.08	0.00	0.00	0.00	0.00

Turnover: 3,392.90
Credit Limit £ 5,000.00

| | | | | Grand Totals: | 7,341.96 | 0.00 | 5,502.36 | 1,839.60 | 0.00 | 0.00 | 0.00 |

(j) Aged debtors

| Date: | 22/08/2017 | **Crazy Hair** | Page: | 1 |
| Time: | 21:53:49 | **Aged Debtors Analysis (Detailed)** | | |

Date From:	01/01/1980		Customer From:	
Date To:	31/05/2017		Customer To:	ZZZZZZZZ
Include future transactions:	No			
Exclude later payments:	No			

** NOTE: All report values are shown in Base Currency, unless otherwise indicated **

| A/C: | 104 | Name: | Alfred Images | Contact: | | Tel: | |

No	Type	Date	Ref	Details	Balance	Future	Current	Period 1	Period 2	Period 3	Older
49	SI	12/05/2017	3354	50 x Brushes	697.20	0.00	697.20	0.00	0.00	0.00	0.00
56	SC	25/05/2017	CN23	Return of Brushes	-67.20	0.00	-67.20	0.00	0.00	0.00	0.00
				Totals:	630.00	0.00	630.00	0.00	0.00	0.00	0.00

Turnover: 2,334.60
Credit Limit £ 8,000.00

| A/C: | 110 | Name: | Figgaro | Contact: | | Tel: | |

No	Type	Date	Ref	Details	Balance	Future	Current	Period 1	Period 2	Period 3	Older
50	SI	13/05/2017	3355	12 x Hairdryers	792.00	0.00	792.00	0.00	0.00	0.00	0.00
				Totals:	792.00	0.00	792.00	0.00	0.00	0.00	0.00

Turnover: 4,540.80
Credit Limit £ 6,500.00

| A/C: | 118 | Name: | Blades | Contact: | | Tel: | |

No	Type	Date	Ref	Details	Balance	Future	Current	Period 1	Period 2	Period 3	Older
51	SI	15/05/2017	3356	8 x Wigs	2,266.99	0.00	2,266.99	0.00	0.00	0.00	0.00
				Totals:	2,266.99	0.00	2,266.99	0.00	0.00	0.00	0.00

Turnover: 4,033.56
Credit Limit £ 6,100.00

| A/C: | 122 | Name: | Hair Studio | Contact: | | Tel: | |

No	Type	Date	Ref	Details	Balance	Future	Current	Period 1	Period 2	Period 3	Older
53	SI	18/05/2017	3357	12 x Brushes	1,714.94	0.00	1,714.94	0.00	0.00	0.00	0.00
75	SP	21/05/2017	CANCEL	Cancelled Cheque	681.60	0.00	681.60	0.00	0.00	0.00	0.00
				Totals:	2,396.54	0.00	2,396.54	0.00	0.00	0.00	0.00

Turnover: 2,110.72
Credit Limit £ 5,000.00

| A/C: | 138 | Name: | Ribbons and Curls | Contact: | | Tel: | |

No	Type	Date	Ref	Details	Balance	Future	Current	Period 1	Period 2	Period 3	Older
5	SI	12/04/2017	3123	Opening Balance	391.20	0.00	0.00	391.20	0.00	0.00	0.00
48	SI	12/05/2017	3353	10 x Colours	169.20	0.00	169.20	0.00	0.00	0.00	0.00
				Totals:	560.40	0.00	169.20	391.20	0.00	0.00	0.00

Turnover: 532.20
Credit Limit £ 5,000.00

| | | | | Grand Totals: | 6,645.93 | 0.00 | 6,254.73 | 391.20 | 0.00 | 0.00 | 0.00 |

(k) Nominal Ledger Activity Report: Bank Current Account and Petty Cash Account

| Date: | 22/08/2017 | | | Crazy Hair | | | | Page: | 1 |
| Time: | 21:55:03 | | | Nominal Activity | | | | | |

| Date From: | 01/01/1980 | | N/C From: | |
| Date To: | 31/05/2017 | | N/C To: | 99999999 |

| Transaction From: | 1 |
| Transaction To: | 99,999,999 |

| N/C: | 1200 | | Name: | Bank Current Account | | | | | Account Balance: | | 55,459.24 DR |

No	Type	Date	Account	Ref	Details	Dept	T/C	Value	Debit	Credit	V	B
14	JD	01/05/2017	1200	O/Bal	Opening Balance	0	T9	54,210.81	54,210.81		-	-
62	BR	20/05/2017	1200	1001	Staff Purchase - Brush	0	T1	21.00	21.00		N	R
63	SR	20/05/2017	104	183001	Sales Receipt	0	T9	1,809.60	1,809.60		-	R
64	SR	21/05/2017	118	654255	Sales Receipt	0	T9	2,144.40	2,144.40		-	R
65	SR	21/05/2017	110	BACS	Sales Receipt	0	T9	3,880.80	3,880.80		-	R
66	SR	21/05/2017	122	CANCEL	Sales Receipt	0	T9	681.60	681.60		-	R
67	PP	31/05/2017	1185	163455	Purchase Payment	0	T9	102.00		102.00	-	N
68	PP	31/05/2017	1134	163456	Purchase Payment	0	T9	4,454.40		4,454.40	-	N
69	PP	31/05/2017	1165	163457	Purchase Payment	0	T9	818.40		818.40	-	N
70	BP	31/05/2017	1200	DD/STO	KH & Sons	0	T9	500.00		500.00	-	R
74	JC	24/05/2017	1200	JH12	Being the transfer of cash for	0	T9	440.00		440.00	-	R
75	SP	21/05/2017	122	CANCEL	Cancelled Cheque	0	T9	681.60		681.60	-	R
76	JC	31/05/2017	1200	TRF01	Bank Transfer	0	T9	30.52		30.52	-	R
78	BP	24/05/2017	1200	DD	Coopers Union	0	T9	168.00		168.00	-	R
79	BP	31/05/2017	1200	DD	Electricity	0	T9	66.94		66.94	-	R
80	BP	31/05/2017	1200		Charges incurred	0	T2	27.11		27.11	N	R
							Totals:		62,748.21	7,288.97		
							History Balance:		55,459.24			

| N/C: | 1230 | | Name: | Petty Cash | | | | | Account Balance: | | 185.69 DR |

No	Type	Date	Account	Ref	Details	Dept	T/C	Value	Debit	Credit	V	B
16	JD	01/05/2017	1230	O/Bal	Opening Balance	0	T9	200.00	200.00		-	-
71	CP	19/05/2017	1230	CSH 86	Petty Cash	0	T1	40.32		40.32	N	-
72	CP	20/05/2017	1230	CSH 87	Petty Cash	0	T9	4.51		4.51	-	-
77	JD	31/05/2017	1230	TRF01	Bank Transfer	0	T9	30.52	30.52		-	-
							Totals:		230.52	44.83		
							History Balance:		185.69			

(l) Bank Reconciliation Report (reconciled transactions)

| Date: | 22/08/2017 | | | Crazy Hair | | | Page: | 1 |
| Time: | 21:57:21 | | | Bank Reconciled Transactions | | | | |

Bank Reconciled On: 31/05/2017

No	Type	Date	A/C	N/C	Dept	Ref	Details	Net	Tax	T/C
14	JD	01/05/2017	1200	1200	0	O/Bal	Opening Balance	54,210.81	0.00	T9
62	BR	20/05/2017	1200	4000	0	1001	Staff Purchase - Brush	17.50	3.50	T1
63	SR	20/05/2017	104	1200	0	183001	Sales Receipt	1,809.60	0.00	T9
64	SR	21/05/2017	118	1200	0	654255	Sales Receipt	2,144.40	0.00	T9
65	SR	21/05/2017	110	1200	0	BACS	Sales Receipt	3,880.80	0.00	T9
66	SR	21/05/2017	122	1200	0	CANCEL	Sales Receipt	681.60	0.00	T9
70	BP	31/05/2017	1200	7100	0	DD/STO	KH & Sons	500.00	0.00	T9
74	JC	24/05/2017	1200	1200	0	JH12	Being the transfer of cash for	440.00	0.00	T9
75	SP	21/05/2017	122	1200	0	CANCEL	Cancelled Cheque	681.60	0.00	T9
76	JC	31/05/2017	1200	1200	0	TRF01	Bank Transfer	30.52	0.00	T9
78	BP	24/05/2017	1200	7104	0	DD	Coopers Union	168.00	0.00	T9
79	BP	31/05/2017	1200	7200	0	DD	Electricity	66.94	0.00	T9
80	BP	31/05/2017	1200	7901	0		Charges incurred	27.11	0.00	T2

PRACTICE PAPER 3

SHOES 4U ANSWERS

TASK 3.4

(a) Customer Address List

| Date: | 22/08/2017 | | Shoes 4U | | Page: | 1 |
| Time: | 22:34:40 | | **Customer Address List** | | | |

Customer From:
Customer To: ZZZZZZZZ

A/C	Name & Address	Contact Name	Telephone	Fax
SL186	Beckers Gate Ltd. Butchergate Carlisle Cumbria C41 1SG			
SL213	Eaton Bowls Club Seaton Street St Neots Cambs PE19 8EF			
SL302	Jones Footwear Scotby Village Carlisle Cumbria C44 8BP			
SL307	Dickens Ladies Footwear 17 Royal Square Bleachfield North Yorkshire YO87 9AD			

(b) Supplier Address List

| Date: | 22/08/2017 | | Shoes 4U | | Page: | 1 |
| Time: | 22:29:19 | | **Supplier Address List** | | | |

Supplier From:
Supplier To: ZZZZZZZZ

A/C	Name	Contact	Telephone	Fax
PL112	Bootsy & Smudge Ltd. Factory Road Stilton Cambs PE7 3RP			
PL168	Briggsthorpe Boots Long Buckby Wharf Long Buckby Northhampton NN4 9UW			
PL172	Gallows Fashion 18 The Crescent Pickford Cambs PE7 8QV			
PL173	Dickens Ladies Footwear 17 Royal Square Bleachfield North Yorkshire YO87 9AD			

(c) Period Trial Balance Report

Date: 22/08/2017	**Shoes 4U**	Page: 1
Time: 22:29:55	**Period Trial Balance**	

To Period: Month 12, December 2017

N/C	Name	Debit	Credit
0010	Freehold Property	72,000.00	
0040	Furniture and Fixtures	9,000.00	
0050	Motor Vehicles	7,500.00	
1100	Debtors Control Account	10,386.27	
1200	Bank Current Account	14,363.00	
1210	Bank Deposit Account	5,000.00	
1230	Petty Cash	200.00	
2100	Creditors Control Account		47,048.26
2200	Sales Tax Control Account		3,402.35
2201	Purchase Tax Control Account	1,130.00	
3000	Capital		30,000.00
3260	Drawings	600.00	
4000	Sales - Men's Footwear		79,320.00
4001	Sales - Ladies Footwear		43,210.00
4002	Cash Sales		6,798.00
5000	Purchases - Men's Footwear	55,432.00	
5001	Purchases - Ladies Footwear	23,410.00	
6201	Advertising	7,231.00	
7100	Rent	1,263.00	
7200	Electricity	567.34	
7502	Telephone	866.00	
7504	Office Stationery	830.00	
	Totals:	209,778.61	209,778.61

TASK 8

Remittance advices

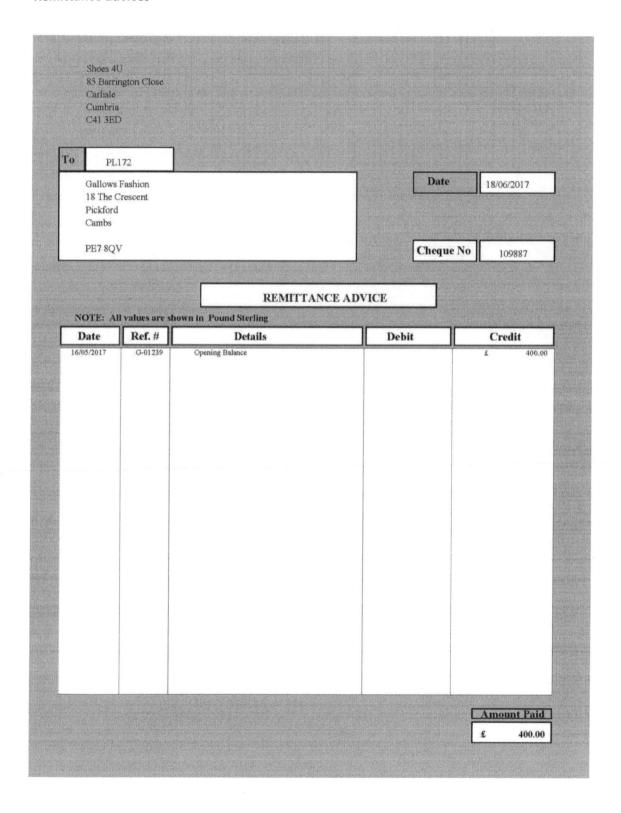

Shoes 4U
85 Barrington Close
Carlisle
Cumbria
C41 3ED

To	PL172

Gallows Fashion
18 The Crescent
Pickford
Cambs

PE7 8QV

Date	18/06/2017

Cheque No	109887

REMITTANCE ADVICE

NOTE: All values are shown in Pound Sterling

Date	Ref. #	Details	Debit	Credit
16/05/2017	G-01239	Opening Balance		£ 400.00

Amount Paid
£ 400.00

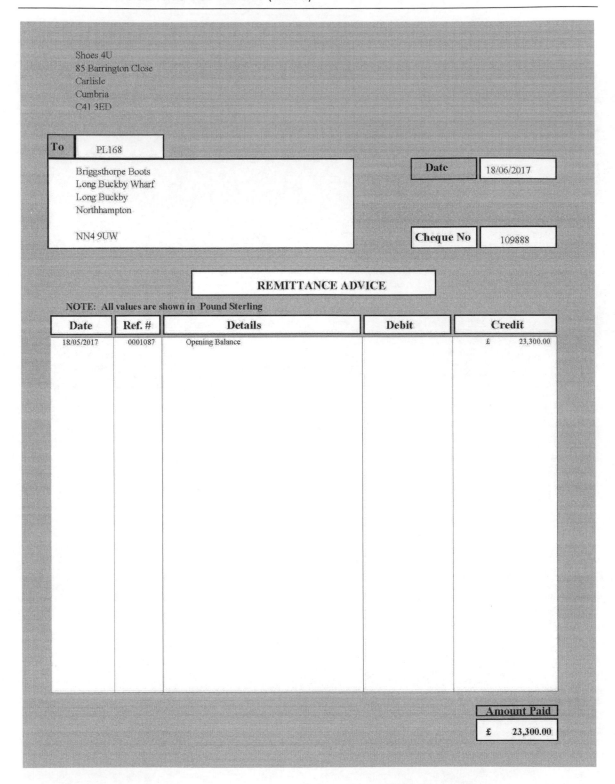

Shoes 4U
85 Barrington Close
Carlisle
Cumbria
C41 3ED

To	PL168

Briggsthorpe Boots
Long Buckby Wharf
Long Buckby
Northhampton

NN4 9UW

Date	18/06/2017

Cheque No	109888

REMITTANCE ADVICE

NOTE: All values are shown in Pound Sterling

Date	Ref. #	Details	Debit	Credit
18/05/2017	0001087	Opening Balance		£ 23,300.00

Amount Paid	
£	23,300.00

TASK 9.1

Screen shot to show setting up the recurring entry

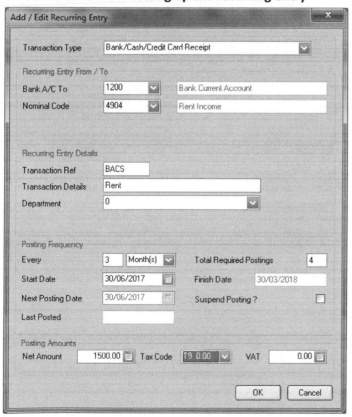

Add / Edit Recurring Entry

Transaction Type	Bank/Cash/Credit Card Payment

Recurring Entry From / To

Bank A/C	1200	Bank Current Account
Nominal Code	7200	Electricity

Recurring Entry Details

Transaction Ref	STO
Transaction Details	ECBE Ltd
Department	0

Posting Frequency

Every	3 Month(s)	Total Required Postings	4
Start Date	25/06/2017	Finish Date	25/03/2018
Next Posting Date	25/06/2017	Suspend Posting ?	☐
Last Posted			

Posting Amounts

Net Amount	193.00	Tax Code T9 0.00	VAT 0.00

OK   Cancel

TASK 9.2

Screen shot to show setting up the recurring entry

Add / Edit Recurring Entry

Transaction Type	Bank/Cash/Credit Card Receipt

Recurring Entry From / To

Bank A/C To	1200	Bank Current Account
Nominal Code	4904	Rent Income

Recurring Entry Details

Transaction Ref	BACS
Transaction Details	Rent
Department	0

Posting Frequency

Every	3 Month(s)	Total Required Postings	4
Start Date	30/06/2017	Finish Date	30/03/2018
Next Posting Date	30/06/2017	Suspend Posting ?	☐
Last Posted			

Posting Amounts

Net Amount	1500.00	Tax Code T9 0.00	VAT 0.00

OK   Cancel

TASK 16

(1) Period Trial Balance Report

| Date: | 22/08/2017 | | Shoes 4U | | Page: | 1 |
| Time: | 23:00:39 | | **Period Trial Balance** | | | |

To Period: Month 12, December 2017

N/C	Name	Debit	Credit
0010	Freehold Property	72,000.00	
0040	Furniture and Fixtures	9,000.00	
0050	Motor Vehicles	7,500.00	
1100	Debtors Control Account	5,212.56	
1200	Bank Current Account		2,531.18
1210	Bank Deposit Account	5,000.00	
1230	Petty Cash	200.00	
2100	Creditors Control Account		29,948.26
2200	Sales Tax Control Account		4,439.43
2201	Purchase Tax Control Account	2,232.25	
3000	Capital		30,000.00
3260	Drawings	3,800.00	
4000	Sales - Men's Footwear		81,669.66
4001	Sales - Ladies Footwear		46,045.75
4002	Cash Sales		6,798.00
4904	Rent Income		1,500.00
5000	Purchases - Men's Footwear	60,432.00	
5001	Purchases - Ladies Footwear	23,910.00	
6201	Advertising	7,231.00	
7100	Rent	1,263.00	
7200	Electricity	760.34	
7502	Telephone	866.00	
7504	Office Stationery	841.25	
7901	Bank Charges	50.00	
8100	Bad Debt Write Off	2,623.98	
8205	Refreshments	9.90	
	Totals:	202,932.28	202,932.28

(2) Sales Day Book

| Date: | 22/08/2017 | | Shoes 4U | | Page: | 1 |
| Time: | 23:01:05 | | **Day Books: Customer Invoices (Detailed)** | | | |

| Date From: | 01/01/1980 | | | Customer From: | |
| Date To: | 31/12/2019 | | | Customer To: | ZZZZZZZZ |

| Transaction From: | 1 | | | N/C From: | |
| Transaction To: | 99,999,999 | | | N/C To: | 99999999 |

| Dept From: | 0 | |
| Dept To: | 999 | |

Tran No.	Type	Date	A/C Ref	N/C	Inv Ref	Dept.	Details	Net Amount	Tax Amount	T/C	Gross Amount	V	B
1	SI	22/05/2017	SL186	9998	1613	0	Opening Balance	4,811.88	0.00	T9	4,811.88	-	-
2	SI	10/05/2017	SL213	9998	1582	0	Opening Balance	961.98	0.00	T9	961.98	-	-
3	SI	28/05/2017	SL302	9998	1596	0	Opening Balance	3,828.75	0.00	T9	3,828.75	-	-
4	SI	21/05/2017	SL307	9998	1601	0	Opening Balance	783.66	0.00	T9	783.66	-	-
49	SI	04/06/2017	SL186	4000	1622	0	Mens footwear	450.00	90.00	T1	540.00	N	-
50	SI	06/06/2017	SL213	4000	1623	0	Mens footwear	1,385.00	277.00	T1	1,662.00	N	-
51	SI	14/06/2017	SL307	4000	1624	0	Mens footwear	450.00	90.00	T1	540.00	N	-
52	SI	14/06/2017	SL307	4001	1624	0	Ladies footwear	1,850.00	370.00	T1	2,220.00	N	-
53	SI	17/06/2017	SL302	4001	1625	0	Ladies footwear	1,175.75	235.15	T1	1,410.90	N	-
							Totals:	15,697.02	1,062.15		16,759.17		

(3) Customer Activity Report

Date:	22/08/2017			Shoes 4U						Page:	1	
Time:	23:01:23			**Customer Activity (Detailed)**								

Date From:	01/01/1980						Customer From:			
Date To:	30/06/2017						Customer To:	ZZZZZZZZ		
Transaction From:	1						N/C From:			
Transaction To:	99,999,999						N/C To:	99999999		
Inc b/fwd transaction:	No						Dept From:	0		
Exc later payment:	No						Dept To:	999		

** NOTE: All report values are shown in Base Currency, unless otherwise indicated **

A/C: SL186   Name: Beckers Gate Ltd.   Contact: Tel:

No	Type	Date	Ref	N/C	Details	Dept	T/C	Value	O/S	Debit	Credit	V	B
1	SI	22/05/2017	1613	9998	Opening Balance	0	T9	4,811.88		4,811.88		-	-
49	SI	04/06/2017	1622	4000	Mens footwear	0	T1	540.00 *	540.00	540.00		N	-
60	SR	11/06/2017	199846	1200	Sales Receipt	0	T9	4,811.88			4,811.88	-	R
					Totals:			540.00	540.00	5,351.88	4,811.88		

Amount Outstanding	540.00
Amount Paid this period	4,811.88
Credit Limit £	5,000.00
Turnover YTD	5,261.88

A/C: SL213   Name: Eaton Bowls Club   Contact: Tel:

No	Type	Date	Ref	N/C	Details	Dept	T/C	Value	O/S	Debit	Credit	V	B
2	SI	10/05/2017	1582	9998	Opening Balance	0	T9	961.98		961.98		-	-
50	SI	06/06/2017	1623	4000	Mens footwear	0	T1	1,662.00		1,662.00		N	-
61	SR	14/06/2017	CANCEL	1200	Sales Receipt	0	T9	961.98			961.98	-	R
74	SP	14/06/2017	CANCEL	1200	Cancelled Cheque	0	T9	961.98		961.98		-	R
75	SC	30/06/2017	BADDBT	8100	Bad Debt Write Off	0	T9	2,623.98			2,623.98	-	-
					Totals:			0.00	0.00	3,585.96	3,585.96		

Amount Outstanding	0.00
Amount Paid this period	0.00
Credit Limit £	3,000.00
Turnover YTD	2,346.98

A/C: SL302   Name: Jones Footwear   Contact: Tel:

No	Type	Date	Ref	N/C	Details	Dept	T/C	Value	O/S	Debit	Credit	V	B
3	SI	28/05/2017	1596	9998	Opening Balance	0	T9	3,828.75		3,828.75		-	-
53	SI	17/06/2017	1625	4001	Ladies footwear	0	T1	1,410.90 *	1,410.90	1,410.90		N	-
62	SR	14/06/2017		1200	Sales Receipt	0	T9	3,828.75			3,828.75	-	R
					Totals:			1,410.90	1,410.90	5,239.65	3,828.75		

Amount Outstanding	1,410.90
Amount Paid this period	3,828.75
Credit Limit £	6,000.00
Turnover YTD	5,004.50

A/C: SL307   Name: Dickens Ladies Footwear   Contact: Tel:

No	Type	Date	Ref	N/C	Details	Dept	T/C	Value	O/S	Debit	Credit	V	B
4	SI	21/05/2017	1601	9998	Opening Balance	0	T9	783.66 *	783.66	783.66		-	-
51	SI	14/06/2017	1624	4000	Mens footwear	0	T1	540.00 *	540.00	540.00		N	-
52	SI	14/06/2017	1624	4001	Ladies footwear	0	T1	2,220.00 *	2,220.00	2,220.00		N	-
54	SC	08/06/2017	CR10	4001	Returned Ladies Footwear	0	T1	-282.00 *	-282.00		282.00	N	-
					Totals:			3,261.66	3,261.66	3,543.66	282.00		

Amount Outstanding	3,261.66
Amount Paid this period	0.00
Credit Limit £	11,000.00
Turnover YTD	2,848.66

(4) Supplier Activity Report

Date:	22/08/2017	**Shoes 4U**	Page: 1
Time:	23:01:49	**Supplier Activity (Detailed)**	

Date From:	01/01/1980	Supplier From:	
Date To:	30/06/2017	Supplier To:	ZZZZZZZZ
Transaction From:	1	N/C From:	
Transaction To:	99,999,999	N/C To:	99999999
Inc b/fwd transaction:	No	Dept From:	0
Exc later payment:	No	Dept To:	999

** NOTE: All report values are shown in Base Currency, unless otherwise indicated **

A/C:	PL112	Name:	Bootsy & Smudge Ltd.		Contact:				Tel:			

No	Type	Date	Ref	N/C	Details	Dept	T/C	Value	O/S	Debit	Credit	V	B
5	PI	22/05/2017	B/468	9998	Opening Balance	0	T9	2,881.26 *	2,881.26		2,881.26	-	-
55	PI	02/06/2017		5001	Ladies footwear	0	T1	360.00 *	360.00		360.00	N	-
58	PI	13/06/2017		5001	Ladies footwear	0	T1	240.00 *	240.00		240.00	N	-
					Totals:			3,481.26	3,481.26	0.00	3,481.26		

Amount Outstanding	3,481.26
Amount paid this period	0.00
Credit Limit £	4,000.00
Turnover YTD	3,381.26

A/C:	PL168	Name:	Briggsthorpe Boots		Contact:				Tel:			

No	Type	Date	Ref	N/C	Details	Dept	T/C	Value	O/S	Debit	Credit	V	B
6	PI	18/05/2017	0001087	9998	Opening Balance	0	T9	43,200.00 p	19,900.00		43,200.00	-	-
56	PI	10/06/2017		5000	Mens footwear	0	T1	3,000.00 *	3,000.00		3,000.00	N	-
64	PP	18/06/2017	109888	1200	Purchase Payment	0	T9	23,300.00	0.00	23,300.00		-	R
					Totals:			22,900.00	22,900.00	23,300.00	46,200.00		

Amount Outstanding	22,900.00
Amount paid this period	23,300.00
Credit Limit £	50,000.00
Turnover YTD	45,700.00

A/C:	PL172	Name:	Gallows Fashion		Contact:				Tel:			

No	Type	Date	Ref	N/C	Details	Dept	T/C	Value	O/S	Debit	Credit	V	B
7	PI	16/05/2017	G-01239	9998	Opening Balance	0	T9	400.00	0.00		400.00	-	-
57	PI	12/06/2017		5000	Mens footwear	0	T1	3,000.00 *	3,000.00		3,000.00	N	-
63	PP	18/06/2017	109887	1200	Purchase Payment	0	T9	400.00	0.00	400.00		-	N
					Totals:			3,000.00	3,000.00	400.00	3,400.00		

Amount Outstanding	3,000.00
Amount paid this period	400.00
Credit Limit £	2,000.00
Turnover YTD	2,900.00

A/C:	PL173	Name:	Dickens Ladies Footwear		Contact:				Tel:			

No	Type	Date	Ref	N/C	Details	Dept	T/C	Value	O/S	Debit	Credit	V	B
8	PI	16/05/2017	06345	9998	Opening Balance	0	T9	567.00 *	567.00		567.00	-	-
					Totals:			567.00	567.00	0.00	567.00		

Amount Outstanding	567.00
Amount paid this period	0.00
Credit Limit £	2,000.00
Turnover YTD	567.00

(5) Aged Creditors Report (detailed)

| Date: | 22/08/2017 | | | | Shoes 4U | | | | Page: | 1 |

Date: 22/08/2017 **Time:** 23:02:10

Shoes 4U

Page: 1

Aged Creditors Analysis (Detailed)

Date From:	01/01/1980		Supplier From:	
Date To:	30/06/2017		Supplier To:	ZZZZZZZZ

Include future transactions: No
Exclude later payments: No

** NOTE: All report values are shown in Base Currency, unless otherwise indicated **

A/C: PL112   Name: Bootsy & Smudge Ltd.   Contact: Tel:

No.	Type	Date	Ref	Details	Balance	Future	Current	Period 1	Period 2	Period 3	Older
5	PI	22/05/2017	B/468	Opening Balance	2,881.26	0.00	0.00	2,881.26	0.00	0.00	0.00
55	PI	02/06/2017		Ladies footwear	360.00	0.00	360.00	0.00	0.00	0.00	0.00
58	PI	13/06/2017		Ladies footwear	240.00	0.00	240.00	0.00	0.00	0.00	0.00
				Totals:	3,481.26	0.00	600.00	2,881.26	0.00	0.00	0.00

Turnover: 3,381.26
Credit Limit £ 4,000.00

A/C: PL168   Name: Briggsthorpe Boots   Contact: Tel:

No.	Type	Date	Ref	Details	Balance	Future	Current	Period 1	Period 2	Period 3	Older
6	PI	18/05/2017	0001087	Opening Balance	19,900.00	0.00	0.00	19,900.00	0.00	0.00	0.00
56	PI	10/06/2017		Mens footwear	3,000.00	0.00	3,000.00	0.00	0.00	0.00	0.00
				Totals:	22,900.00	0.00	3,000.00	19,900.00	0.00	0.00	0.00

Turnover: 45,700.00
Credit Limit £ 50,000.00

A/C: PL172   Name: Gallows Fashion   Contact: Tel:

No.	Type	Date	Ref	Details	Balance	Future	Current	Period 1	Period 2	Period 3	Older
57	PI	12/06/2017		Mens footwear	3,000.00	0.00	3,000.00	0.00	0.00	0.00	0.00
				Totals:	3,000.00	0.00	3,000.00	0.00	0.00	0.00	0.00

Turnover: 2,900.00
Credit Limit £ 2,000.00

A/C: PL173   Name: Dickens Ladies Footwear   Contact: Tel:

No.	Type	Date	Ref	Details	Balance	Future	Current	Period 1	Period 2	Period 3	Older
8	PI	16/05/2017	06345	Opening Balance	567.00	0.00	0.00	567.00	0.00	0.00	0.00
				Totals:	567.00	0.00	0.00	567.00	0.00	0.00	0.00

Turnover: 567.00
Credit Limit £ 2,000.00

| | | | | Grand Totals: | 29,948.26 | 0.00 | 6,600.00 | 23,348.26 | 0.00 | 0.00 | 0.00 |

(6) Aged Debtors Report (detailed)

Date:	22/08/2017		Shoes 4U				Page:	1
Time:	23:02:33		**Aged Debtors Analysis (Detailed)**					

Date From:	01/01/1980			Customer From:	
Date To:	30/06/2017			Customer To:	ZZZZZZZZ
Include future transactions:	No				
Exclude later payments:	No				

** NOTE: All report values are shown in Base Currency, unless otherwise indicated **

A/C: SL186   Name: Beckers Gate Ltd.   Contact: Tel:

No	Type	Date	Ref	Details	Balance	Future	Current	Period 1	Period 2	Period 3	Older
49	SI	04/06/2017	1622	Mens footwear	540.00	0.00	540.00	0.00	0.00	0.00	0.00
				Totals:	540.00	0.00	540.00	0.00	0.00	0.00	0.00

Turnover: 5,261.88
Credit Limit £   5,000.00

A/C: SL302   Name: Jones Footwear   Contact: Tel:

No	Type	Date	Ref	Details	Balance	Future	Current	Period 1	Period 2	Period 3	Older
53	SI	17/06/2017	1625	Ladies footwear	1,410.90	0.00	1,410.90	0.00	0.00	0.00	0.00
				Totals:	1,410.90	0.00	1,410.90	0.00	0.00	0.00	0.00

Turnover: 5,004.50
Credit Limit £   6,000.00

A/C: SL307   Name: Dickens Ladies Footwear   Contact: Tel:

No	Type	Date	Ref	Details	Balance	Future	Current	Period 1	Period 2	Period 3	Older
4	SI	21/05/2017	1601	Opening Balance	783.66	0.00	0.00	783.66	0.00	0.00	0.00
51	SI	14/06/2017	1624	Mens footwear	2,760.00	0.00	2,760.00	0.00	0.00	0.00	0.00
54	SC	08/06/2017	CR10	Returned Ladies	-282.00	0.00	-282.00	0.00	0.00	0.00	0.00
				Totals:	3,261.66	0.00	2,478.00	783.66	0.00	0.00	0.00

Turnover: 2,848.66
Credit Limit £   11,000.00

				Grand Totals:	5,212.56	0.00	4,428.90	783.66	0.00	0.00	0.00

(7) Nominal Ledger Activity Report for Bank Current Account and Petty Cash Account

| Date: | 22/08/2017 | | | | Shoes 4U | | | | | Page: | 1 | |
| Time: | 23:03:21 | | | | **Nominal Activity** | | | | | | | |

| Date From: | 01/01/1980 | | | | | | | N/C From: | | | | |
| Date To: | 30/06/2017 | | | | | | | N/C To: | 99999999 | | | |

| Transaction From: | 1 | | | | | | | | | | | |
| Transaction To: | 99,999,999 | | | | | | | | | | | |

| N/C: | 1200 | Name: | Bank Current Account | | | | | Account Balance: | | 2,531.18 CR |

No	Type	Date	Account	Ref	Details	Dept	T/C	Value	Debit	Credit	V	B
15	JD	01/06/2017	1200	O/Bal	Opening Balance	0	T9	19,363.00	19,363.00		-	-
47	JC	01/06/2017	1200	TRF01	Bank Transfer	0	T9	5,000.00		5,000.00	-	R
59	BR	23/06/2017	1200	F027	Cash Sale - Mens footwear	0	T1	77.59	77.59		N	R
60	SR	11/06/2017	SL186	199846	Sales Receipt	0	T9	4,811.88	4,811.88		-	R
61	SR	14/06/2017	SL213	CANCEL	Sales Receipt	0	T9	961.98	961.98		-	R
62	SR	14/06/2017	SL302		Sales Receipt	0	T9	3,828.75	3,828.75		-	R
63	PP	18/06/2017	PL172	109887	Purchase Payment	0	T9	400.00		400.00	-	N
64	PP	18/06/2017	PL168	109888	Purchase Payment	0	T9	23,300.00		23,300.00	-	R
65	BP	25/06/2017	1200	STO	ECBE Ltd	0	T9	193.00		193.00	-	R
66	BR	30/06/2017	1200	BACS	Rent	0	T9	1,500.00	1,500.00		-	R
69	JC	10/06/2017	1200	TRF02	Bank Transfer	0	T9	23.40		23.40	-	R
72	JC	25/06/2017	1200	209	Being transfer of cash for personal	0	T9	3,200.00		3,200.00	-	R
73	BR	22/06/2017	1200	DC03	Cash Sale - Ladies footwear	0	T1	54.00	54.00		N	R
74	SP	14/06/2017	SL213	CANCEL	Cancelled Cheque	0	T9	961.98		961.98	-	R
76	BP	25/06/2017	1200		Charges incurred	0	T2	50.00		50.00	N	R
							Totals:		30,597.20	33,128.38		
							History Balance:			2,531.18		

| N/C: | 1230 | Name: | Petty Cash | | | | | Account Balance: | | 200.00 DR |

No	Type	Date	Account	Ref	Details	Dept	T/C	Value	Debit	Credit	V	B
17	JD	01/06/2017	1230	O/Bal	Opening Balance	0	T9	200.00	200.00		-	-
67	CP	05/06/2017	1230	010	Refreshments	0	T0	9.90		9.90	N	-
68	CP	10/06/2017	1230	011	Office Stationery	0	T1	13.50		13.50	N	-
70	JD	10/06/2017	1230	TRF02	Bank Transfer	0	T9	23.40	23.40		-	-
							Totals:		223.40	23.40		
							History Balance:			200.00		

(8) Audit trail

| Date: | 22/08/2017 | | | | | Shoes 4U | | | | | Page: | 1 |
| Time: | 23:04:01 | | | | | **Audit Trail (Detailed)** | | | | | | |

| Date From: | 01/01/1980 | | | | | | | | Customer From: | | |
| Date To: | 31/12/2019 | | | | | | | | Customer To: | ZZZZZZZ | |

| Transaction From: | 1 | | | | | | | | Supplier From: | | |
| Transaction To: | 99,999,999 | | | | | | | | Supplier To: | ZZZZZZZ | |

| Exclude Deleted Tran: | No |

No	Type	A/C	N/C	Dept	Details	Date	Ref	Net	Tax	T/C	Pd	Paid	V	B	Bank Rec. Date
1	SI	SL186				22/05/2017	1613	4,811.88	0.00		Y	4,811.88			
		1	9998	0	Opening Balance			4,811.88	0.00	T9		4,811.88	-		
					4811.88 from SR 60	11/06/2017	199846					4,811.88			
2	SI	SL213				10/05/2017	1582	961.98	0.00		Y	961.98			
		2	9998	0	Opening Balance			961.98	0.00	T9		961.98	-		
					961.98 from SR 61	14/06/2017						961.98			
3	SI	SL302				28/05/2017	1596	3,828.75	0.00		Y	3,828.75			
		3	9998	0	Opening Balance			3,828.75	0.00	T9		3,828.75	-		
					3828.75 from SR 62	14/06/2017						3,828.75			
4	SI	SL307				21/05/2017	1601	783.66	0.00		N	0.00			
		4	9998	0	Opening Balance			783.66	0.00	T9		0.00	-		
5	PI	PL112				22/05/2017	B/468	2,881.26	0.00		N	0.00			
		5	9998	0	Opening Balance			2,881.26	0.00	T9		0.00	-		
6	PI	PL168				18/05/2017	0001087	43,200.00	0.00		N	23,300.00			
		6	9998	0	Opening Balance			43,200.00	0.00	T9		23,300.00	-		
					23300.00 from PP 64	18/06/2017	109888					23,300.00			
7	PI	PL172				16/05/2017	G-01239	400.00	0.00		Y	400.00			
		7	9998	0	Opening Balance			400.00	0.00	T9		400.00	-		
					400.00 from PP 63	18/06/2017	109887					400.00			
8	PI	PL173				16/05/2017	06345	567.00	0.00		N	0.00			
		8	9998	0	Opening Balance			567.00	0.00	T9		0.00	-		
9	JD	0010				01/06/2017	O/Bal	72,000.00	0.00		Y	72,000.00			
		9	0010	0	Opening Balance			72,000.00	0.00	T9		72,000.00	-		
10	JC	9998				01/06/2017	O/Bal	72,000.00	0.00		Y	72,000.00	-		

| Date: | 22/08/2017 | | | | | | | Shoes 4U | | | | | | Page: | 2 |
| Time: | 23:04:01 | | | | | | | Audit Trail (Detailed) | | | | | | | |

No	Type	A/C	N/C	Dept	Details	Date	Ref	Net	Tax	T/C	Pd	Paid	V	B	Bank Rec. Date
10		10	9998	0	Opening Balance			72,000.00	0.00	T9		72,000.00	-		
11	JD	0050				01/06/2017	O/Bal	7,500.00	0.00		Y	7,500.00	-		
11			0050	0	Opening Balance			7,500.00	0.00	T9		7,500.00	-		
12	JC	9998				01/06/2017	O/Bal	7,500.00	0.00		Y	7,500.00	-		
12			9998	0	Opening Balance			7,500.00	0.00	T9		7,500.00	-		
13	JD	0040				01/06/2017	O/Bal	9,000.00	0.00		Y	9,000.00	-		
13			0040	0	Opening Balance			9,000.00	0.00	T9		9,000.00	-		
14	JC	9998				01/06/2017	O/Bal	9,000.00	0.00		Y	9,000.00	-		
14			9998	0	Opening Balance			9,000.00	0.00	T9		9,000.00	-		
15	JD	1200				01/06/2017	O/Bal	19,363.00	0.00		Y	19,363.00	-		30/06/2017
15			1200	0	Opening Balance			19,363.00	0.00	T9		19,363.00	-		
16	JC	9998				01/06/2017	O/Bal	19,363.00	0.00		Y	19,363.00	-		
16			9998	0	Opening Balance			19,363.00	0.00	T9		19,363.00	-		
17	JD	1230				01/06/2017	O/Bal	200.00	0.00		Y	200.00	-		30/06/2017
17			1230	0	Opening Balance			200.00	0.00	T9		200.00	-		
18	JC	9998				01/06/2017	O/Bal	200.00	0.00		Y	200.00	-		
18			9998	0	Opening Balance			200.00	0.00	T9		200.00	-		
19	JC	2200				01/06/2017	O/Bal	3,402.35	0.00		Y	3,402.35	-		
19			2200	0	Opening Balance			3,402.35	0.00	T9		3,402.35	-		
20	JD	9998				01/06/2017	O/Bal	3,402.35	0.00		Y	3,402.35	-		
20			9998	0	Opening Balance			3,402.35	0.00	T9		3,402.35	-		
21	JD	2201				01/06/2017	O/Bal	1,130.00	0.00		Y	1,130.00	-		
21			2201	0	Opening Balance			1,130.00	0.00	T9		1,130.00	-		
22	JC	9998				01/06/2017	O/Bal	1,130.00	0.00		Y	1,130.00	-		
22			9998	0	Opening Balance			1,130.00	0.00	T9		1,130.00	-		
23	JC	3000				01/06/2017	O/Bal	30,000.00	0.00		Y	30,000.00	-		
23			3000	0	Opening Balance			30,000.00	0.00	T9		30,000.00	-		
24	JD	9998				01/06/2017	O/Bal	30,000.00	0.00		Y	30,000.00	-		
24			9998	0	Opening Balance			30,000.00	0.00	T9		30,000.00	-		

| Date: | 22/08/2017 | | | | | | | Shoes 4U | | | | | | Page: | 3 |
| Time: | 23:04:01 | | | | | | | Audit Trail (Detailed) | | | | | | | |

No	Type	A/C	N/C	Dept	Details	Date	Ref	Net	Tax	T/C	Pd	Paid	V	B	Bank Rec. Date
25	JD	3260				01/06/2017	O/Bal	600.00	0.00		Y	600.00	-		
25			3260	0	Opening Balance			600.00	0.00	T9		600.00	-		
26	JC	9998				01/06/2017	O/Bal	600.00	0.00		Y	600.00	-		
26			9998	0	Opening Balance			600.00	0.00	T9		600.00	-		
27	JC	4000				01/06/2017	O/Bal	79,320.00	0.00		Y	79,320.00	-		
27			4000	0	Opening Balance			79,320.00	0.00	T9		79,320.00	-		
28	JD	9998				01/06/2017	O/Bal	79,320.00	0.00		Y	79,320.00	-		
28			9998	0	Opening Balance			79,320.00	0.00	T9		79,320.00	-		
29	JC	4001				01/06/2017	O/Bal	43,210.00	0.00		Y	43,210.00	-		
29			4001	0	Opening Balance			43,210.00	0.00	T9		43,210.00	-		
30	JD	9998				01/06/2017	O/Bal	43,210.00	0.00		Y	43,210.00	-		
30			9998	0	Opening Balance			43,210.00	0.00	T9		43,210.00	-		
31	JC	4002				01/06/2017	O/Bal	6,798.00	0.00		Y	6,798.00	-		
31			4002	0	Opening Balance			6,798.00	0.00	T9		6,798.00	-		
32	JD	9998				01/06/2017	O/Bal	6,798.00	0.00		Y	6,798.00	-		
32			9998	0	Opening Balance			6,798.00	0.00	T9		6,798.00	-		
33	JD	5000				01/06/2017	O/Bal	55,432.00	0.00		Y	55,432.00	-		
33			5000	0	Opening Balance			55,432.00	0.00	T9		55,432.00	-		
34	JC	9998				01/06/2017	O/Bal	55,432.00	0.00		Y	55,432.00	-		
34			9998	0	Opening Balance			55,432.00	0.00	T9		55,432.00	-		
35	JD	5001				01/06/2017	O/Bal	23,410.00	0.00		Y	23,410.00	-		
35			5001	0	Opening Balance			23,410.00	0.00	T9		23,410.00	-		
36	JC	9998				01/06/2017	O/Bal	23,410.00	0.00		Y	23,410.00	-		
36			9998	0	Opening Balance			23,410.00	0.00	T9		23,410.00	-		
37	JD	6201				01/06/2017	O/Bal	7,231.00	0.00		Y	7,231.00	-		
37			6201	0	Opening Balance			7,231.00	0.00	T9		7,231.00	-		
38	JC	9998				01/06/2017	O/Bal	7,231.00	0.00		Y	7,231.00	-		
38			9998	0	Opening Balance			7,231.00	0.00	T9		7,231.00	-		
39	JD	7502				01/06/2017	O/Bal	866.00	0.00		Y	866.00	-		

KAPLAN PUBLISHING

Date: 22/08/2017
Time: 23:04:01

Shoes 4U
Audit Trail (Detailed)

Page: 4

No	Type	A/C	N/C	Dept	Details	Date	Ref	Net	Tax	T/C	Pd	Paid	V	B	Bank Rec. Date
		39	7502	0	Opening Balance			866.00	0.00	T9		866.00	-		
40	JC	9998				01/06/2017	O/Bal	866.00	0.00		Y	866.00			
		40	9998	0	Opening Balance			866.00	0.00	T9		866.00	-		
41	JD	7100				01/06/2017	O/Bal	1,263.00	0.00		Y	1,263.00	-		
		41	7100	0	Opening Balance			1,263.00	0.00	T9		1,263.00	-		
42	JC	9998				01/06/2017	O/Bal	1,263.00	0.00		Y	1,263.00			
		42	9998	0	Opening Balance			1,263.00	0.00	T9		1,263.00	-		
43	JD	7200				01/06/2017	O/Bal	567.34	0.00		Y	567.34	-		
		43	7200	0	Opening Balance			567.34	0.00	T9		567.34	-		
44	JC	9998				01/06/2017	O/Bal	567.34	0.00		Y	567.34			
		44	9998	0	Opening Balance			567.34	0.00	T9		567.34	-		
45	JD	7504				01/06/2017	O/Bal	830.00	0.00		Y	830.00	-		
		45	7504	0	Opening Balance			830.00	0.00	T9		830.00	-		
46	JC	9998				01/06/2017	O/Bal	830.00	0.00		Y	830.00	-		
		46	9998	0	Opening Balance			830.00	0.00	T9		830.00	-		
47	JC	1200				01/06/2017	TRF01	5,000.00	0.00		Y	5,000.00		R	30/06/2017
		47	1200	0	Bank Transfer			5,000.00	0.00	T9		5,000.00	-		
48	JD	1210				01/06/2017	TRF01	5,000.00	0.00		Y	5,000.00	N		
		48	1210	0	Bank Transfer			5,000.00	0.00	T9		5,000.00	-		
49	SI	SL186				04/06/2017	1622	450.00	90.00		N	0.00	-		
		49	4000	0	Mens footwear			450.00	90.00	T1		0.00	N		
50	SI	SL213				06/06/2017	1623	1,385.00	277.00		Y	1,662.00			
		50	4000	0	Mens footwear			1,385.00	277.00	T1		1,662.00	N		
					1662.00 from SC 75	30/06/2017	BADDBT					1,662.00			
51	SI	SL307				14/06/2017	1624	2,300.00	460.00		N	0.00	-		
		51	4000	0	Mens footwear			450.00	90.00	T1		0.00	N		
		52	4001	0	Ladies footwear			1,850.00	370.00	T1		0.00	N		
53	SI	SL302				17/06/2017	1625	1,175.75	235.15		N	0.00	-		
		53	4001	0	Ladies footwear			1,175.75	235.15	T1		0.00	N		
54	SC	SL307				08/06/2017	CR10	235.00	47.00		N	0.00	-		

Date: 22/08/2017
Time: 23:04:01

Shoes 4U
Audit Trail (Detailed)

Page: 5

No	Type	A/C	N/C	Dept	Details	Date	Ref	Net	Tax	T/C	Pd	Paid	V	B	Bank Rec. Date
		54	4001	0	Returned Ladies			235.00	47.00	T1		0.00	N		
55	PI	PL112				02/06/2017		300.00	60.00		N	0.00	-		
		55	5001	0	Ladies footwear			300.00	60.00	T1		0.00	N		
56	PI	PL168				10/06/2017		2,500.00	500.00		N	0.00	-		
		56	5000	0	Mens footwear			2,500.00	500.00	T1		0.00	N		
57	PI	PL172				12/06/2017		2,500.00	500.00		N	0.00	-		
		57	5000	0	Mens footwear			2,500.00	500.00	T1		0.00	N		
58	PI	PL112				13/06/2017		200.00	40.00		N	0.00	-		
		58	5001	0	Ladies footwear			200.00	40.00	T1		0.00	N		
59	BR	1200				23/06/2017	F027	64.66	12.93		Y	77.59		R	30/06/2017
		59	4000	0	Cash Sale – Mens			64.66	12.93	T1		77.59	N		
60	SR	SL186				11/06/2017	199846	4,811.88	0.00		Y	4,811.88		R	30/06/2017
		60	1200	0	Sales Receipt			4,811.88	0.00	T9		4,811.88	-		
					4811.88 to SI 1	11/06/2017	1613					4,811.88			
61	SR	SL213				14/06/2017	CANCEL	961.98	0.00		Y	961.98		R	30/06/2017
		61	1200	0	Sales Receipt			961.98	0.00	T9		961.98	-		
					961.98 to SI 2	14/06/2017	1582					961.98			
62	SR	SL302				14/06/2017		3,828.75	0.00		Y	3,828.75		R	30/06/2017
		62	1200	0	Sales Receipt			3,828.75	0.00	T9		3,828.75	-		
					3828.75 to SI 3	14/06/2017	1596					3,828.75			
63	PP	PL172				18/06/2017	109887	400.00	0.00		Y	400.00	N		
		63	1200	0	Purchase Payment			400.00	0.00	T9		400.00	-		
					400.00 to PI 7	18/06/2017	G-01239					400.00			
64	PP	PL168				18/06/2017	109888	23,300.00	0.00		Y	23,300.00		R	30/06/2017
		64	1200	0	Purchase Payment			23,300.00	0.00	T9		23,300.00	-		
					23300.00 to PI 6	18/06/2017	0001087					23,300.00			
65	BP	1200				25/06/2017	STO	193.00	0.00		Y	193.00		R	30/06/2017
		65	7200	0	ECBE Ltd			193.00	0.00	T9		193.00	-		
66	BR	1200				30/06/2017	BACS	1,500.00	0.00		Y	1,500.00		R	30/06/2017
		66	4904	0	Rent			1,500.00	0.00	T9		1,500.00	-		

| Date: | 22/08/2017 | | | | | Shoes 4U | | | | | | Page: | 6 |
| Time: | 23:04:01 | | | | | **Audit Trail (Detailed)** | | | | | | | |

No	Type	A/C	N/C	Dept	Details	Date	Ref	Net	Tax	T/C	Pd	Paid	V	B	Bank Rec. Date
67	CP	1230				05/06/2017	010	9.90	0.00		Y	9.90	-		
		67	8205	0	Refreshments			9.90	0.00	T0		9.90	N		
68	CP	1230				10/06/2017	011	11.25	2.25		Y	13.50	-		
		68	7504	0	Office Stationery			11.25	2.25	T1		13.50	N		
69	JC	1200				10/06/2017	TRF02	23.40	0.00		Y	23.40	R		30/06/2017
		69	1200	0	Bank Transfer			23.40	0.00	T9		23.40	-		
70	JD	1230				10/06/2017	TRF02	23.40	0.00		Y	23.40	-		
		70	1230	0	Bank Transfer			23.40	0.00	T9		23.40	-		
71	JD	3260				25/06/2017	209	3,200.00	0.00		Y	3,200.00	-		
		71	3260	0	Being transfer of			3,200.00	0.00	T9		3,200.00	-		
72	JC	1200				25/06/2017	209	3,200.00	0.00		Y	3,200.00	R		30/06/2017
		72	1200	0	Being transfer of			3,200.00	0.00	T9		3,200.00	-		
73	BR	1200				22/06/2017	DC03	45.00	9.00		Y	54.00	R		30/06/2017
		73	4001	0	Cash Sale - Ladies			45.00	9.00	T1		54.00	N		
74	SP	SL213				14/06/2017	CANCEL	961.98	0.00		Y	961.98	R		30/06/2017
		74	1200	0	Cancelled Cheque 961.98 from SC 75	30/06/2017	BADDBT	961.98	0.00	T9		961.98	-		
												961.98			
75	SC	SL213				30/06/2017	BADDBT	2,623.98	0.00		Y	2,623.98	-		
		75	8100	0	Bad Debt Write Off			2,623.98	0.00	T9		2,623.98	-		
					1662.00 to SI 50	30/06/2017	1623					1,662.00			
					961.98 to SP 74	30/06/2017	CANCEL					961.98			
76	BP	1200				25/06/2017		50.00	0.00		Y	50.00	R		30/06/2017
		76	7901	0	Charges incurred			50.00	0.00	T2		50.00	N		

(9) Bank Reconciliation (Reconciled transactions)

| Date: | 22/08/2017 | Shoes 4U | Page: | 1 |
| Time: | 23:04:33 | **Bank Reconciled Transactions** | | |

Bank Reconciled On: 30/06/2017

No	Type	Date	A/C	N/C	Dept	Ref	Details	Net	Tax	T/C
15	JD	01/06/2017	1200	1200	0	O/Bal	Opening Balance	19,363.00	0.00	T9
47	JC	01/06/2017	1200	1200	0	TRF01	Bank Transfer	5,000.00	0.00	T9
59	BR	23/06/2017	1200	4000	0	F027	Cash Sale - Mens footwear	64.66	12.93	T1
60	SR	11/06/2017	SL186	1200	0	199846	Sales Receipt	4,811.88	0.00	T9
61	SR	14/06/2017	SL213	1200	0	CANCEL	Sales Receipt	961.98	0.00	T9
62	SR	14/06/2017	SL302	1200	0		Sales Receipt	3,828.75	0.00	T9
64	PP	18/06/2017	PL168	1200	0	109888	Purchase Payment	23,300.00	0.00	T9
65	BP	25/06/2017	1200	7200	0	STO	ECBE Ltd	193.00	0.00	T9
66	BR	30/06/2017	1200	4904	0	BACS	Rent	1,500.00	0.00	T9
69	JC	10/06/2017	1200	1200	0	TRF02	Bank Transfer	23.40	0.00	T9
72	JC	25/06/2017	1200	1200	0	209	Being transfer of cash for	3,200.00	0.00	T9
73	BR	22/06/2017	1200	4001	0	DC03	Cash Sale - Ladies footwear	45.00	9.00	T1
74	SP	14/06/2017	SL213	1200	0	CANCEL	Cancelled Cheque	961.98	0.00	T9
76	BP	25/06/2017	1200	7901	0		Charges incurred	50.00	0.00	T2

PRACTICE PAPER 4

SPORTS GEAR ANSWERS

TASK 3.3

(a) Customer Address List

| Date: | 23/08/2017 | | Sports Gear | | Page: | 1 |
| Time: | 10:18:41 | | Customer Address List | | | |

Customer From:
Customer To: ZZZZZZZZ

A/C	Name & Address	Contact Name	Telephone	Fax
SL01	J Hollingham 56 Glencoe Avenue Gants Hill Ilford Essex IG1 6FR			
SL02	Paul McCallum 34 St Albans Road Seven Kings Essex IG7 8DS			
SL03	Kerry Jenkins 34 Gloucester Road Gillingham Kent ME14 3TL			
SL04	Harry Bucket 54 Dale Road Harrogate North Yorks YO2 3HN			
SL05	Evelyn Rose 98 Crabtree Drive Bromley Kent DA3 6AY			

(b) Supplier Address List

| Date: | 23/08/2017 | | Sports Gear | | Page: | 1 |
| Time: | 10:19:03 | | Supplier Address List | | | |

Supplier From:
Supplier To: ZZZZZZZZ

A/C	Name	Contact	Telephone	Fax
PL01	Radcliffe & Sons Orient House Lower Clapham London E1 2RH			
PL02	Tennison Bros White Cottage London WC1 6YD			
PL03	Skipton & Co 22 Chatsworth Lane Water Square London EC1V 6NJ			
PL04	Evelyn Rose 98 Crabtree Drive Bromley Kent DA3 6AY			

(c) Period Trial Balance Report

Date:	23/08/2017					
Time:	10:17:01					

Sports Gear

Period Trial Balance

Page: 1

To Period: Month 12, December 2017

N/C	Name	Debit	Credit
0030	Office Equipment	8,430.00	
0040	Furniture and Fixtures	18,000.00	
0050	Motor Vehicles	15,500.00	
1100	Debtors Control Account	8,445.46	
1200	Bank Current Account	3,325.40	
1230	Petty Cash	300.00	
2100	Creditors Control Account		8,914.14
2200	Sales Tax Control Account		3,458.00
2201	Purchase Tax Control Account	1,120.00	
3000	Capital		52,000.00
3260	Drawings	1,294.00	
4000	Sales - Tennis Racquets		13,266.78
4001	Sales - Exercise Bikes		22,310.00
4002	Sales - Golf Clubs		9,543.00
4003	Sales - Fishing Rods		5,644.00
5000	Purchases - Tennis Racquets	21,354.00	
5001	Purchases - Exercise Bikes	25,610.00	
5002	Purchases - Golf Clubs	5,475.00	
5003	Purchases - Fishing Rods	4,796.00	
7200	Electricity	496.06	
7504	Office Stationery	430.00	
7803	Postage	560.00	
	Totals:	115,135.92	115,135.92

TASK 8

Remittance advices

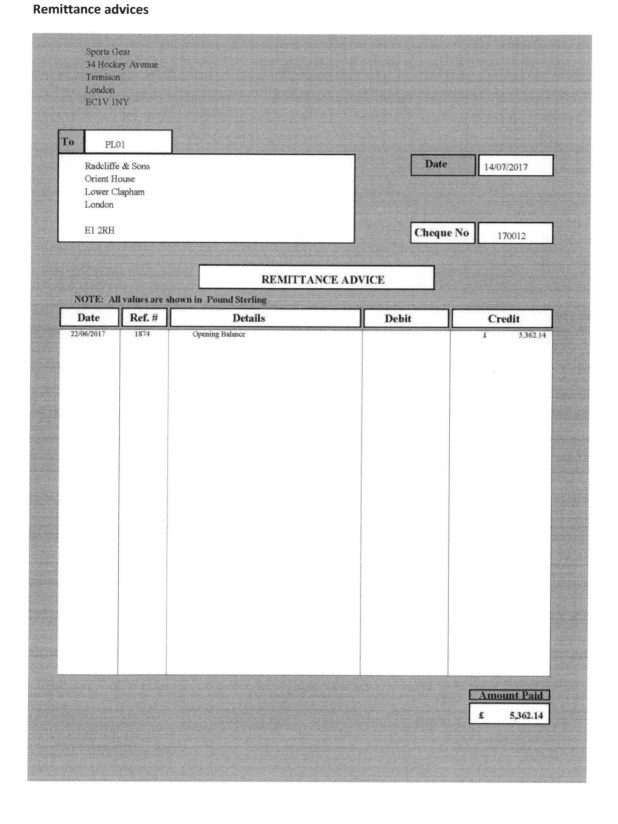

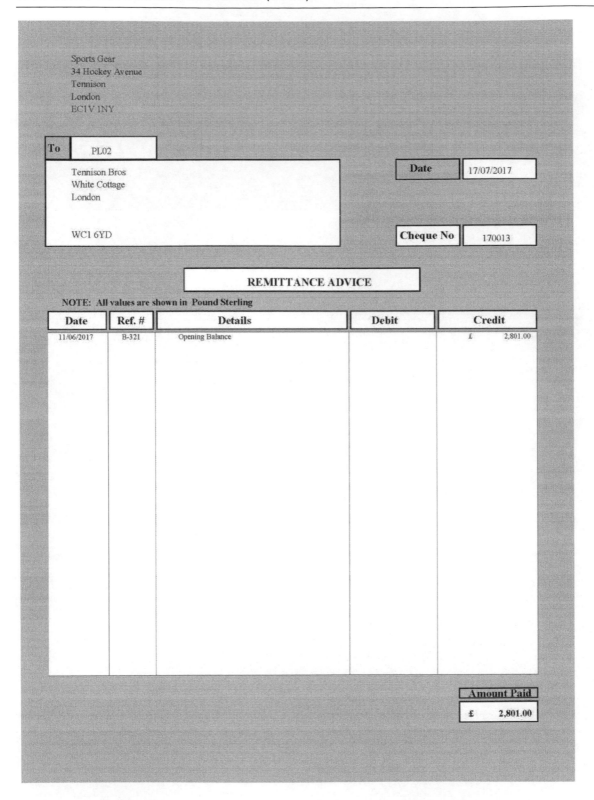

Sports Gear
34 Hockey Avenue
Tennison
London
EC1V 1NY

To	PL02

Tennison Bros
White Cottage
London

WC1 6YD

Date	17/07/2017

Cheque No	170013

REMITTANCE ADVICE

NOTE: All values are shown in Pound Sterling

Date	Ref. #	Details	Debit	Credit
11/06/2017	B-321	Opening Balance		£ 2,801.00

Amount Paid
£   2,801.00

TASK 9

Screen shot to show setting up the recurring entry

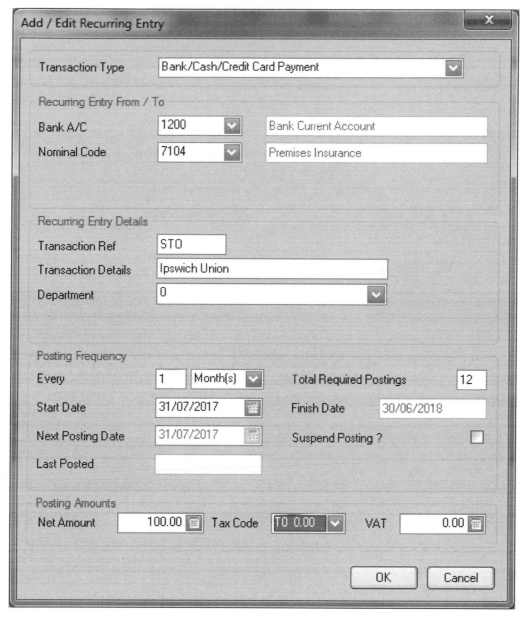

TASK 12

Screen shot to show updated customer details

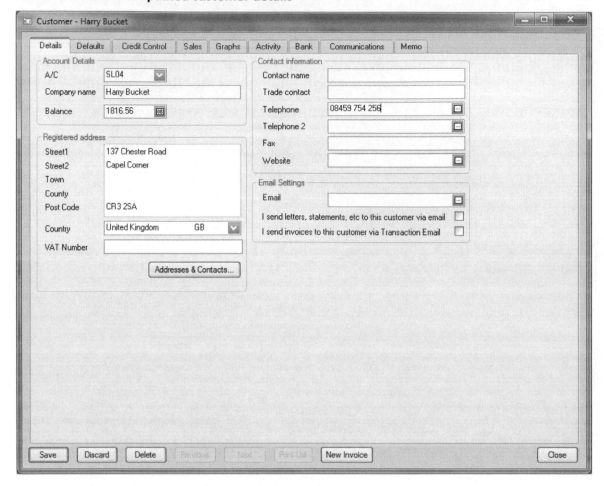

TASK 21

Customer address list

Date: 23/08/2017

Time: 10:48:42

Sports Gear

Customer Address List

Page: 1

Customer From:
Customer To: ZZZZZZZZZ

A/C	Name & Address	Contact Name	Telephone	Fax
SL01	J Hollingham 56 Glencoe Avenue Gants Hill Ilford Essex IG1 6FR			
SL02	Paul McCallum 34 St Albans Road Seven Kings Essex IG7 8DS			
SL03	Kerry Jenkins 34 Gloucester Road Gillingham Kent ME14 3TL			
SL04	Harry Bucket 137 Chester Road Capel Corner CR3 2SA		08459 754 256	
SL05	Evelyn Rose 98 Crabtree Drive Bromley Kent DA3 6AY			

Period Trial Balance Report

Date: 23/08/2017

Time: 10:53:14

Sports Gear

Period Trial Balance

Page: 1

To Period: Month 12, December 2017

N/C	Name	Debit	Credit
0030	Office Equipment	8,430.00	
0040	Furniture and Fixtures	18,000.00	
0050	Motor Vehicles	15,500.00	
1100	Debtors Control Account	3,176.64	
1200	Bank Current Account	4,166.44	
1230	Petty Cash	300.00	
2100	Creditors Control Account		2,468.46
2200	Sales Tax Control Account		5,027.40
2201	Purchase Tax Control Account	1,662.62	
3000	Capital		52,000.00
3260	Drawings	4,735.00	
4000	Sales - Tennis Racquets		16,318.50
4001	Sales - Exercise Bikes		25,222.47
4002	Sales - Golf Clubs		11,101.80
4003	Sales - Fishing Rods		5,968.00
5000	Purchases - Tennis Racquets	21,904.00	
5001	Purchases - Exercise Bikes	25,930.00	
5002	Purchases - Golf Clubs	6,303.55	
5003	Purchases - Fishing Rods	5,467.00	
7104	Premises Insurance	100.00	
7200	Electricity	496.06	
7504	Office Stationery	449.90	
7803	Postage	938.55	
7901	Bank Charges	32.19	
8100	Bad Debt Write Off	514.68	
	Totals:	**118,106.63**	**118,106.63**

Sales Day Book

Date: 23/08/2017
Time: 10:49:16

Sports Gear

Day Books: Customer Invoices (Detailed)

Page: 1

| Date From: | 01/01/1980 | | Customer From: | |
| Date To: | 31/12/2019 | | Customer To: | ZZZZZZZZ |

| Transaction From: | 1 | | N/C From: | |
| Transaction To: | 99,999,999 | | N/C To: | 99999999 |

| Dept From: | 0 |
| Dept To: | 999 |

Tran No.	Type	Date	A/C Ref	N/C	Inv Ref	Dept.	Details	Net Amount	Tax Amount	T/C	Gross Amount	V	B
1	SI	12/06/2017	SL01	9998	1001	0	Opening Balance	3,462.12	0.00	T9	3,462.12	-	-
2	SI	10/06/2017	SL02	9998	0087	0	Opening Balance	514.68	0.00	T9	514.68	-	-
3	SI	08/06/2017	SL03	9998	0093	0	Opening Balance	758.34	0.00	T9	758.34	-	-
4	SI	12/06/2017	SL04	9998	1003	0	Opening Balance	2,767.34	0.00	T9	2,767.34	-	-
5	SI	12/06/2017	SL05	9998	1004	0	Opening Balance	942.98	0.00	T9	942.98	-	-
50	SI	04/07/2017	SL01	4000	1052	0	20 Tennis Racquets	882.00	176.40	T1	1,058.40	N	-
51	SI	04/07/2017	SL01	4001	1052	0	10 Exercise Bikes	1,023.60	204.72	T1	1,228.32	N	-
52	SI	04/07/2017	SL01	4003	1052	0	6 Fishing Rods	324.00	64.80	T1	388.80	N	-
53	SI	06/07/2017	SL03	4000	1053	0	3 Tennis Racquets	132.30	26.46	T1	158.76	N	-
54	SI	08/07/2017	SL04	4002	1054	0	18 Golf Clubs	1,513.80	302.76	T1	1,816.56	N	-
							Totals:	12,321.16	775.14		13,096.30		

Purchase Day Book

Date: 23/08/2017
Time: 00:11:39

Sports Gear

Day Books: Supplier Invoices (Detailed)

Page: 1

| Date From: | 01/01/1980 | | Supplier From: | |
| Date To: | 31/12/2019 | | Supplier To: | ZZZZZZZZ |

| Transaction From: | 1 | | N/C From: | |
| Transaction To: | 99,999,999 | | N/C To: | 99999999 |

| Dept From: | 0 |
| Dept To: | 999 |

Tran No.	Type	Date	A/C Ref	N/C	Inv Ref	Dept	Details	Net Amount	Tax Amount	T/C	Gross Amount	V	B
6	PI	22/06/2017	PL01	9998	1874	0	Opening Balance	5,362.14	0.00	T9	5,362.14	-	-
7	PI	11/06/2017	PL02	9998	B-321	0	Opening Balance	2,801.00	0.00	T9	2,801.00	-	-
8	PI	11/06/2017	PL03	9998	1087	0	Opening Balance	501.00	0.00	T9	501.00	-	-
9	PI	18/06/2017	PL04	9998	A193	0	Opening Balance	250.00	0.00	T9	250.00	-	-
56	PI	03/07/2017	PL01	5000	1099	0	Tennis Racquets	550.00	110.00	T1	660.00	N	-
57	PI	05/07/2017	PL02	5001	B-1147	0	Exercise Bikes	320.00	64.00	T1	384.00	N	-
58	PI	05/07/2017	PL02	7803	B-1147	0	Postage	35.00	0.00	T0	35.00	N	-
59	PI	10/07/2017	PL03	5002	2785	0	Golf Clubs	938.00	187.60	T1	1,125.60	N	-
60	PI	10/07/2017	PL04	5003	A/5698	0	Fishing Rods	671.00	134.20	T1	805.20	N	-
							Totals	11,428.14	495.80		11,923.94		

Customer Activity Report

Date:	23/08/2017		**Sports Gear**		Page:	1
Time:	10:49:42		**Customer Activity (Detailed)**			

Date From:	01/01/1980		Customer From:		
Date To:	31/07/2017		Customer To:	ZZZZZZZZ	
Transaction From:	1		N/C From:		
Transaction To:	99,999,999		N/C To:	99999999	
Inc b/fwd transaction:	No		Dept From:	0	
Exc later payment:	No		Dept To:	999	

** NOTE: All report values are shown in Base Currency, unless otherwise indicated **

A/C:	SL01	Name:	J Hollingham		Contact:				Tel:			

No	Type	Date	Ref	N/C	Details	Dept	T/C	Value	O/S	Debit	Credit	V	B
1	SI	12/06/2017	1001	9998	Opening Balance	0	T9	3,462.12		3,462.12		-	-
50	SI	04/07/2017	1052	4000	20 Tennis Racquets	0	T1	1,058.40		1,058.40		N	-
51	SI	04/07/2017	1052	4001	10 Exercise Bikes	0	T1	1,228.32		1,228.32		N	-
52	SI	04/07/2017	1052	4003	6 Fishing Rods	0	T1	388.80		388.80		N	-
55	SC	17/07/2017	CR34	4001	Return of faulty exercise bike	0	T1	612.75			612.75	N	-
65	SR	19/07/2017		1200	Sales Receipt	0	T9	2,849.37			2,849.37	-	R
77	SR	28/07/2017		1200	Sales Receipt	0	T9	2,675.52			2,675.52	-	R
					Totals:			0.00	0.00	6,137.64	6,137.64		

Amount Outstanding	0.00
Amount Paid this period	5,524.89
Credit Limit £	5,000.00
Turnover YTD	5,181.09

A/C:	SL02	Name:	Paul McCallum		Contact:				Tel:			

No	Type	Date	Ref	N/C	Details	Dept	T/C	Value	O/S	Debit	Credit	V	B
2	SI	10/06/2017	0087	9998	Opening Balance	0	T9	514.68		514.68		-	-
82	SC	31/07/2017	BADDBT	8100	Bad Debt Write Off	0	T9	514.68			514.68	-	-
					Totals:			0.00	0.00	514.68	514.68		

Amount Outstanding	0.00
Amount Paid this period	0.00
Credit Limit £	9,500.00
Turnover YTD	514.68

A/C:	SL03	Name:	Kerry Jenkins		Contact:				Tel:			

No	Type	Date	Ref	N/C	Details	Dept	T/C	Value	O/S	Debit	Credit	V	B
3	SI	08/06/2017	0093	9998	Opening Balance	0	T9	758.34		758.34		-	-
53	SI	06/07/2017	1053	4000	3 Tennis Racquets	0	T1	158.76 *	158.76	158.76		N	-
66	SR	12/07/2017	CANCEL	1200	Sales Receipt	0	T9	758.34			758.34	-	R
81	SP	12/07/2017	CANCEL	1200	Cancelled Cheque	0	T9	758.34	758.34	758.34		-	R
					Totals:			917.10	917.10	1,675.44	758.34		

Amount Outstanding	917.10
Amount Paid this period	0.00
Credit Limit £	8,000.00
Turnover YTD	890.64

A/C:	SL04	Name:	Harry Bucket		Contact:				Tel:	08459 754 256		

No	Type	Date	Ref	N/C	Details	Dept	T/C	Value	O/S	Debit	Credit	V	B
4	SI	12/06/2017	1003	9998	Opening Balance	0	T9	2,767.34		2,767.34		-	-
54	SI	08/07/2017	1054	4002	18 Golf Clubs	0	T1	1,816.56 p	1,316.56	1,816.56		N	-
67	SR	13/07/2017		1200	Sales Receipt	0	T9	2,767.34			2,767.34	-	R
78	SR	28/07/2017		1200	Sales Receipt	0	T9	500.00			500.00	-	R
					Totals:			1,316.56	1,316.56	4,583.90	3,267.34		

Amount Outstanding	1,316.56
Amount Paid this period	3,267.34
Credit Limit £	12,000.00
Turnover YTD	4,281.14

Date:	23/08/2017		**Sports Gear**		Page:	2
Time:	10:49:42		**Customer Activity (Detailed)**			

A/C:	SL05	Name:	Evelyn Rose		Contact:				Tel:			

No	Type	Date	Ref	N/C	Details	Dept	T/C	Value	O/S	Debit	Credit	V	B
5	SI	12/06/2017	1004	9998	Opening Balance	0	T9	942.98 *	942.98	942.98		-	-
					Totals:			942.98	942.98	942.98			

Amount Outstanding	942.98
Amount Paid this period	0.00
Credit Limit £	7,000.00
Turnover YTD	942.98

Supplier Activity Report

Sports Gear
Supplier Activity (Detailed)

Date From:	01/01/1980	Supplier From:
Date To:	31/07/2017	Supplier To: ZZZZZZZZ
Transaction From:	1	N/C From:
Transaction To:	99,999,999	N/C To: 99999999
Inc b/fwd transaction:	No	Dept From: 0
Exc later payment:	No	Dept To: 999

** NOTE: All report values are shown in Base Currency, unless otherwise indicated **

A/C: PL01   Name: Radcliffe & Sons   Contact: Tel:

No	Type	Date	Ref	N/C	Details	Dept	T/C	Value	O/S	Debit	Credit	V	B
6	PI	22/06/2017	1874	9998	Opening Balance	0	T9	5,362.14	0.00		5,362.14	-	-
56	PI	03/07/2017	1099	5000	Tennis Racquets	0	T1	660.00	0.00		660.00	N	-
68	PP	14/07/2017	170012	1200	Purchase Payment	0	T9	5,362.14	0.00	5,362.14		-	N
76	PP	28/07/2017	170015	1200	Purchase Payment	0	T9	660.00	0.00	660.00		-	N
					Totals:			0.00	0.00	6,022.14	6,022.14		

Amount Outstanding	0.00
Amount paid this period	6,022.14
Credit Limit £	15,500.00
Turnover YTD	5,912.14

A/C: PL02   Name: Tennison Bros   Contact: Tel:

No	Type	Date	Ref	N/C	Details	Dept	T/C	Value	O/S	Debit	Credit	V	B
7	PI	11/06/2017	B-321	9998	Opening Balance	0	T9	2,801.00	0.00		2,801.00	-	-
57	PI	03/07/2017	B-1147	5001	Exercise Bikes	0	T1	384.00 *	384.00		384.00	N	-
58	PI	03/07/2017	B-1147	7803	Postage	0	T0	35.00 *	35.00		35.00	N	-
69	PP	17/07/2017	170013	1200	Purchase Payment	0	T9	2,801.00	0.00	2,801.00		-	R
					Totals:			419.00	419.00	2,801.00	3,220.00		

Amount Outstanding	419.00
Amount paid this period	2,801.00
Credit Limit £	11,000.00
Turnover YTD	3,156.00

A/C: PL03   Name: Skipton & Co   Contact: Tel:

No	Type	Date	Ref	N/C	Details	Dept	T/C	Value	O/S	Debit	Credit	V	B
8	PI	11/06/2017	1087	9998	Opening Balance	0	T9	501.00	0.00		501.00	-	-
59	PI	10/07/2017	2785	5002	Golf Clubs	0	T1	1,125.60 *	1,125.60		1,125.60	N	-
61	PC	19/07/2017	CX432	5002	Return of golf clubs	0	T1	131.34 *	-131.34	131.34		N	-
75	PP	28/07/2017	170014	1200	Purchase Payment	0	T9	501.00	0.00	501.00		-	N
					Totals:			994.26	994.26	632.34	1,626.60		

Amount Outstanding	994.26
Amount paid this period	501.00
Credit Limit £	9,000.00
Turnover YTD	1,329.55

A/C: PL04   Name: Evelyn Rose   Contact: Tel:

No	Type	Date	Ref	N/C	Details	Dept	T/C	Value	O/S	Debit	Credit	V	B
9	PI	18/06/2017	A193	9998	Opening Balance	0	T9	250.00 *	250.00		250.00	-	-
60	PI	10/07/2017	A/5698	5003	Fishing Rods	0	T1	805.20 *	805.20		805.20	N	-
					Totals:			1,055.20	1,055.20	0.00	1,055.20		

Amount Outstanding	1,055.20
Amount paid this period	0.00
Credit Limit £	3,000.00
Turnover YTD	921.00

Nominal Ledger Activity Report for Bank Current Account and Petty Cash Account

Date:	23/08/2017		**Sports Gear**		Page:	1
Time:	10:54:04		**Nominal Activity**			

Date From:	01/01/1980	N/C From:	
Date To:	31/07/2017	N/C To:	99999999

Transaction From:	1
Transaction To:	99,999,999

N/C:	1200	Name:	Bank Current Account	Account Balance:	4,166.44 DR

No	Type	Date	Account	Ref	Details	Dept	T/C	Value	Debit	Credit	V	B
16	JD	01/07/2017	1200	O/Bal	Opening Balance	0	T9	3,325.40	3,325.40		-	-
62	BR	13/07/2017	1200	REC101	Cash Sales	0	T1	1,200.00	1,200.00		N	R
63	BR	15/07/2017	1200	REC102	Cash Sales	0	T1	2,879.40	2,879.40		N	R
64	BR	15/07/2017	1200	REC103	Cash Sales	0	T1	1,194.90	1,194.90		N	R
65	SR	19/07/2017	SL01		Sales Receipt	0	T9	2,849.37	2,849.37		-	R
66	SR	12/07/2017	SL03	CANCEL	Sales Receipt	0	T9	758.34	758.34		-	R
67	SR	13/07/2017	SL04		Sales Receipt	0	T9	2,767.34	2,767.34		-	R
68	PP	14/07/2017	PL01	170012	Purchase Payment	0	T9	5,362.14		5,362.14 -		N
69	PP	17/07/2017	PL02	170013	Purchase Payment	0	T9	2,801.00		2,801.00 -		R
70	BP	28/07/2017	1200	DD/STO	Ipswich Union	0	T9	100.00		100.00 -		R
74	JC	25/01/2017	1200	JNL004	Being the transfer of cash for	0	T9	3,441.00		3,441.00 -		R
75	PP	28/07/2017	PL03	170014	Purchase Payment	0	T9	501.00		501.00 -		N
76	PP	28/07/2017	PL01	170015	Purchase Payment	0	T9	660.00		660.00 -		N
77	SR	28/07/2017	SL01		Sales Receipt	0	T9	2,675.52	2,675.52		-	R
78	SR	28/07/2017	SL04		Sales Receipt	0	T9	500.00	500.00		-	R
79	BR	14/07/2017	1200	ST5	Staff Sale	0	T1	50.00	50.00		N	R
80	BR	19/07/2017	1200	CS03	Debit Card	0	T1	54.00	54.00		N	R
81	SP	12/07/2017	SL03	CANCEL	Cancelled Cheque	0	T9	758.34		758.34 -		R
83	BP	31/07/2017	1200		Charges incurred	0	T2	32.19		32.19 N		R
84	JC	31/07/2017	1200	TRF01	Bank Transfer	0	T9	432.16		432.16 -		N

				Totals:	18,254.27	14,087.83
				History Balance:	4,166.44	

N/C:	1230	Name:	Petty Cash	Account Balance:	300.00 DR

No	Type	Date	Account	Ref	Details	Dept	T/C	Value	Debit	Credit	V	B
18	JD	01/07/2017	1230	O/Bal	Opening Balance	0	T9	300.00	300.00		-	-
71	CP	10/07/2017	1230	152	Stationery	0	T0	19.90		19.90 N		-
72	CP	20/07/2017	1230	187	Postage	0	T1	412.26		412.26 N		-
85	JD	31/07/2017	1230	TRF01	Bank Transfer	0	T9	432.16	432.16		-	-

				Totals:	732.16	432.16
				History Balance:	300.00	

Aged Creditors Report

Date:	23/08/2017			Sports Gear				Page:	1	
Time:	10:51:38			**Aged Creditors Analysis (Detailed)**						

Date From:	01/01/1980					Supplier From:	
Date To:	31/07/2017					Supplier To:	ZZZZZZZZ

Include future transactions: No
Exclude later payments: No

** NOTE: All report values are shown in Base Currency, unless otherwise indicated **

A/C: PL02 Name: Tennison Bros Contact: Tel:

No:	Type	Date	Ref	Details	Balance	Future	Current	Period 1	Period 2	Period 3	Older
57	PI	03/07/2017	B-1147	Exercise Bikes	419.00	0.00	419.00	0.00	0.00	0.00	0.00
				Totals:	419.00	0.00	419.00	0.00	0.00	0.00	0.00

Turnover: 3,156.00
Credit Limit £ 11,000.00

A/C: PL03 Name: Skipton & Co Contact: Tel:

No:	Type	Date	Ref	Details	Balance	Future	Current	Period 1	Period 2	Period 3	Older
59	PI	10/07/2017	2785	Golf Clubs	1,125.60	0.00	1,125.60	0.00	0.00	0.00	0.00
61	PC	19/07/2017	CX432	Return of golf clubs	-131.34	0.00	-131.34	0.00	0.00	0.00	0.00
				Totals:	994.26	0.00	994.26	0.00	0.00	0.00	0.00

Turnover: 1,329.55
Credit Limit £ 9,000.00

A/C: PL04 Name: Evelyn Rose Contact: Tel:

No:	Type	Date	Ref	Details	Balance	Future	Current	Period 1	Period 2	Period 3	Older
9	PI	18/06/2017	A193	Opening Balance	250.00	0.00	0.00	250.00	0.00	0.00	0.00
60	PI	10/07/2017	A/5698	Fishing Rods	805.20	0.00	805.20	0.00	0.00	0.00	0.00
				Totals:	1,055.20	0.00	805.20	250.00	0.00	0.00	0.00

Turnover: 921.00
Credit Limit £ 3,000.00

				Grand Totals:	2,468.46	0.00	2,218.46	250.00	0.00	0.00	0.00

Aged Debtors Report

Date:	23/08/2017			Sports Gear				Page:	1	
Time:	10:50:03			**Aged Debtors Analysis (Detailed)**						

Date From:	01/01/1980					Customer From:	
Date To:	31/07/2017					Customer To:	ZZZZZZZZ

Include future transactions: No
Exclude later payments: No

** NOTE: All report values are shown in Base Currency, unless otherwise indicated **

A/C: SL03 Name: Kerry Jenkins Contact: Tel:

No	Type	Date	Ref	Details	Balance	Future	Current	Period 1	Period 2	Period 3	Older
53	SI	06/07/2017	1053	3 Tennis Racquets	158.76	0.00	158.76	0.00	0.00	0.00	0.00
81	SP	12/07/2017	CANCEL	Cancelled Cheque	758.34	0.00	758.34	0.00	0.00	0.00	0.00
				Totals:	917.10	0.00	917.10	0.00	0.00	0.00	0.00

Turnover: 890.64
Credit Limit £ 8,000.00

A/C: SL04 Name: Harry Bucket Contact: Tel: 08459 754 256

No	Type	Date	Ref	Details	Balance	Future	Current	Period 1	Period 2	Period 3	Older
54	SI	08/07/2017	1054	18 Golf Clubs	1,316.56	0.00	1,316.56	0.00	0.00	0.00	0.00
				Totals:	1,316.56	0.00	1,316.56	0.00	0.00	0.00	0.00

Turnover: 4,281.14
Credit Limit £ 12,000.00

A/C: SL05 Name: Evelyn Rose Contact: Tel:

No	Type	Date	Ref	Details	Balance	Future	Current	Period 1	Period 2	Period 3	Older
5	SI	12/06/2017	1004	Opening Balance	942.98	0.00	0.00	942.98	0.00	0.00	0.00
				Totals:	942.98	0.00	0.00	942.98	0.00	0.00	0.00

Turnover: 942.98
Credit Limit £ 7,000.00

				Grand Totals:	3,176.64	0.00	2,233.66	942.98	0.00	0.00	0.00

KAPLAN PUBLISHING

Print Statement for Paul McCallum

Sports Gear
34 Hockey Avenue
Tennison
London
EC1V 1NY

Sports Gear
34 Hockey Avenue
Tennison
London
EC1V 1NY

	SL02
Paul McCallum 34 St Albans Road Seven Kings Essex	31/07/2017
IG7 8DS	1

	SL02
Paul McCallum 34 St Albans Road Seven Kings Essex	31/07/2017
IG7 8DS	1

NOTE: All values are shown in Pound Sterling

NOTE: All values are shown in **Pound Sterling**

10/06/17	0087	Goods/Services	514.68	
31/07/17	BADDBT	Credit		514.68

10/06/17	Goods/Services	514.68	
31/07/17	Credit		514.68

£   0.00   £   0.00   £   0.00   £   0.00   £   0.00

£   0.00

£   0.00

Bank Reconciliation (Reconciled transactions)

Date: 23/08/2017

Time: 10:55:15

Sports Gear

Bank Reconciled Transactions

Page: 1

Bank Reconciled On: 31/07/2017

No	Type	Date	A/C	N/C	Dept	Ref	Details	Net	Tax	T/C
16	JD	01/07/2017	1200	1200	0	O/Bal	Opening Balance	3,325.40	0.00	T9
62	BR	13/07/2017	1200	4000	0	REC101	Cash Sales	1,000.00	200.00	T1
63	BR	15/07/2017	1200	4001	0	REC102	Cash Sales	2,399.50	479.90	T1
64	BR	15/07/2017	1200	4000	0	REC103	Cash Sales	995.75	199.15	T1
65	SR	19/07/2017	SL01	1200	0		Sales Receipt	2,849.37	0.00	T9
66	SR	12/07/2017	SL03	1200	0	CANCEL	Sales Receipt	758.34	0.00	T9
67	SR	13/07/2017	SL04	1200	0		Sales Receipt	2,767.34	0.00	T9
69	PP	17/07/2017	PL02	1200	0	170013	Purchase Payment	2,801.00	0.00	T9
70	BP	28/07/2017	1200	7104	0	DD/STO	Ipswich Union	100.00	0.00	T9
74	JC	25/01/2017	1200	1200	0	JNL004	Being the transfer of cash for	3,441.00	0.00	T9
77	SR	28/07/2017	SL01	1200	0		Sales Receipt	2,675.52	0.00	T9
78	SR	28/07/2017	SL04	1200	0		Sales Receipt	500.00	0.00	T9
79	BR	14/07/2017	1200	4000	0	ST5	Staff Sale	41.67	8.33	T1
80	BR	19/07/2017	1200	4002	0	CS03	Debit Card	45.00	9.00	T1
81	SP	12/07/2017	SL03	1200	0	CANCEL	Cancelled Cheque	758.34	0.00	T9
83	BP	31/07/2017	1200	7901	0		Charges incurred	32.19	0.00	T2

PRACTICE PAPER 5

WAY TO WORK LTD ANSWERS

TASK 3.3

Customer Address List

Date:	23/08/2017	**Way to Work Ltd**		Page:	1
Time:	11:39:59	**Customer Address List**			

Customer From:
Customer To: ZZZZZZZZ

A/C	Name & Address	Contact Name	Telephone	Fax
JP01	Morgan, Smith & Winston City Road Islington London N1 9PL			
JP02	Cyril West Grays West Grays Inn Road London WC1 1LT			
JP03	Wallace & Gromit Ltd 134 Upper Street Islington London N1 2PT			
JP04	Star Paper 66 White Lion Street London N1 5RX			

Supplier Address List

Date:	23/08/2017	**Way to Work Ltd**		Page:	1
Time:	12:52:33	**Supplier Address List**			

Supplier From:
Supplier To: ZZZZZZZZ

A/C	Name	Contact	Telephone	Fax
SP01	Paper Products UK South Down Trading Estate Sheffield S15 4DR			
SP02	Wallace & Gromit Ltd. 134 Upper Street Islington London N1 2PT			
SP03	Whole Office Furniture 176 East Way Leeds LD4 6PP			
SP04	Stationery World 32 Great Portland Road London WC1V 6HH			

Period Trial Balance

| Date: | 23/08/2017 | | **Way to Work Ltd** | | Page: | 1 |
| Time: | 11:39:22 | | **Period Trial Balance** | | | |

To Period: Month 12, December 2017

N/C	Name	Debit	Credit
0040	Furniture and Fixtures	8,000.00	
0050	Motor Vehicles	14,000.00	
1100	Debtors Control Account	9,173.68	
1200	Bank Current Account	4,710.81	
1210	Bank Deposit Account	1,500.00	
1230	Petty Cash	100.00	
2100	Creditors Control Account		18,535.76
3000	Capital		34,000.00
3260	Drawings	1,000.00	
4000	Stationery Sales		903.73
4001	CD Roms Sales		855.00
4002	Printer Accessory Sales		9,842.00
5000	Stationery Purchases	2,400.00	
5001	CD Rom Purchases	210.00	
5002	Printer Accessory Purchases	15,000.00	
7005	Wages and Salaries	5,600.00	
7100	Rent	2,100.00	
7803	General Expenses	342.00	
	Totals:	64,136.49	64,136.49

TASK 8

Remittance advices

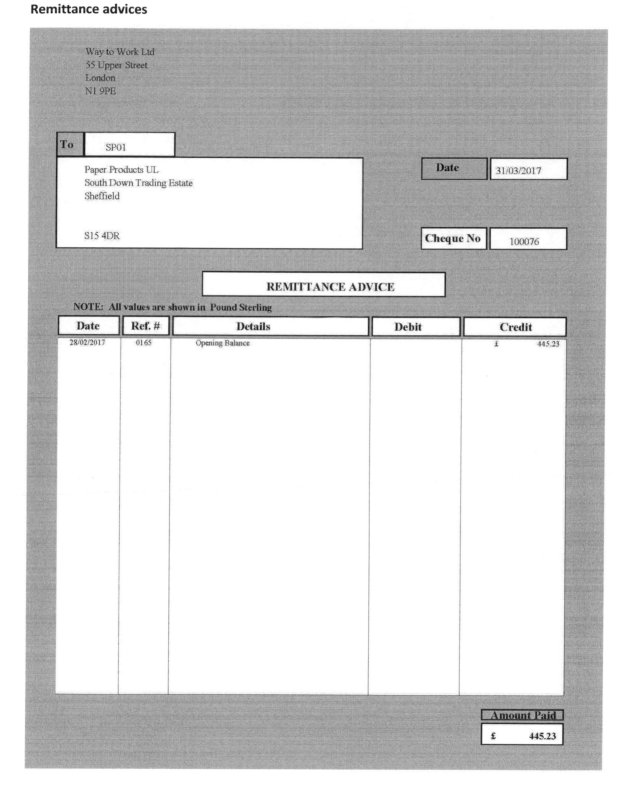

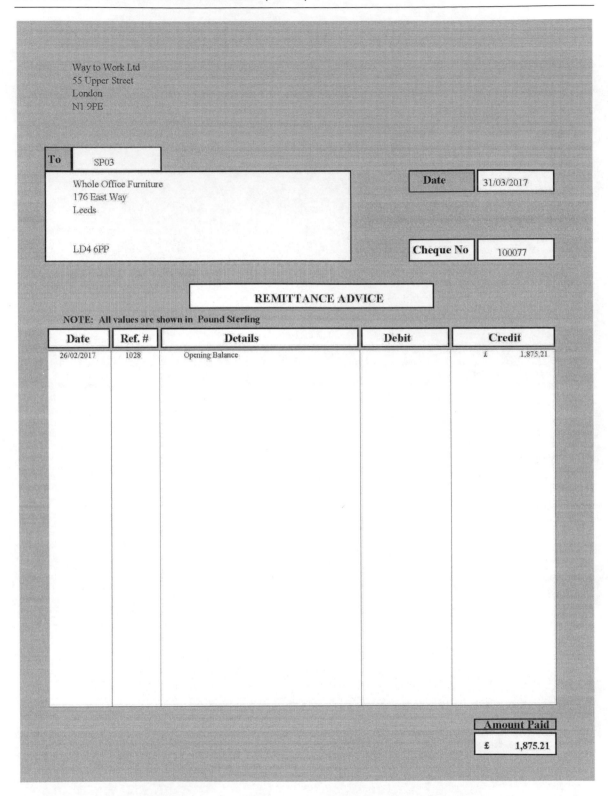

Way to Work Ltd
55 Upper Street
London
N1 9PE

To	SP03

Whole Office Furniture
176 East Way
Leeds

LD4 6PP

Date	31/03/2017

Cheque No	100077

REMITTANCE ADVICE

NOTE: All values are shown in Pound Sterling

Date	Ref. #	Details	Debit	Credit
26/02/2017	1028	Opening Balance		£ 1,875.21

Amount Paid	
£	1,875.21

Way to Work Ltd
55 Upper Street
London
N1 9PE

To	SP04				

Stationery World			Date	31/03/2017
32 Great Portland Road				
London				
WC1V 6HH			Cheque No	100078

REMITTANCE ADVICE

NOTE: All values are shown in Pound Sterling

Date	Ref. #	Details	Debit	Credit
18/02/2017	0187	Opening Balance		£ 9,504.32

Amount Paid	
£	9,504.32

TASK 9

Screen shot to show setting up the recurring entry

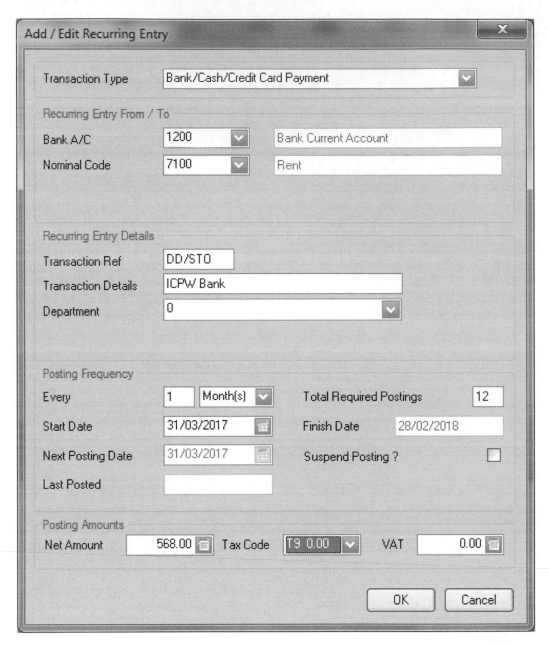

TASK 13

Customer Activity (detailed report)

Date:	23/08/2017		**Way to Work Ltd**		Page:	1
Time:	12:56:02		**Customer Activity (Detailed)**			

Date From:	01/01/1980			Customer From:	
Date To:	31/03/2017			Customer To:	ZZZZZZZZ
Transaction From:	1			N/C From:	
Transaction To:	99,999,999			N/C To:	99999999
Inc b/fwd transaction:	No			Dept From:	0
Exc later payment:	No			Dept To:	999

** NOTE: All report values are shown in Base Currency, unless otherwise indicated **

A/C:	JP01	Name:	Morgan, Smith & Winston		Contact:				Tel:				

No	Type	Date	Ref	N/C	Details	Dept	T/C	Value	O/S	Debit	Credit	V	B
1	SI	14/02/2017	INV021	9998	Opening Balance	0	T9	1,172.34		1,172.34		-	-
43	SI	05/03/2017	INV043	4002	Printer Accessory	0	T1	5,251.20 *	5,251.20	5,251.20		N	-
45	SI	07/03/2017	INV045	4000	Stationery	0	T1	7,452.00 *	7,452.00	7,452.00		N	-
53	SR	15/03/2017		1200	Sales Receipt	0	T9	1,172.34			1,172.34	-	R
					Totals:			12,703.20	12,703.20	13,875.54	1,172.34		

Amount Outstanding	12,703.20
Amount Paid this period	1,172.34
Credit Limit £	7,000.00
Turnover YTD	11,758.34

A/C:	JP02	Name:	Cyril West		Contact:				Tel:				

No	Type	Date	Ref	N/C	Details	Dept	T/C	Value	O/S	Debit	Credit	V	B
2	SI	22/02/2017	INV045	9998	Opening Balance	0	T9	2,954.00		2,954.00		-	-
41	SI	03/03/2017	INV041	4000	Stationery	0	T9	936.00 *	936.00	936.00		N	-
54	SR	17/03/2017		1200	Sales Receipt	0	T9	2,954.00			2,954.00	-	R
					Totals:			936.00	936.00	3,890.00	2,954.00		

Amount Outstanding	936.00
Amount Paid this period	2,954.00
Credit Limit £	8,500.00
Turnover YTD	3,734.00

A/C:	JP03	Name:	Wallace & Gromit Ltd.		Contact:				Tel:				

No	Type	Date	Ref	N/C	Details	Dept	T/C	Value	O/S	Debit	Credit	V	B
3	SI	18/02/2017	INV033	9998	Opening Balance	0	T9	3,180.00 *	3,180.00	3,180.00		-	-
44	SI	07/03/2017	INV044	4002	Printer Accessory	0	T1	549.60 *	549.60	549.60		N	-
					Totals:			3,729.60	3,729.60	3,729.60			

Amount Outstanding	3,729.60
Amount Paid this period	0.00
Credit Limit £	17,000.00
Turnover YTD	3,638.00

A/C:	JP04	Name:	Star Paper		Contact:				Tel:				

No	Type	Date	Ref	N/C	Details	Dept	T/C	Value	O/S	Debit	Credit	V	B
4	SI	22/02/2017	INV34	9998	Opening Balance	0	T9	1,867.34		1,867.34		-	-
42	SI	03/03/2017	INV042	4001	CD Roms	0	T1	1,105.20 *	1,105.20	1,105.20		N	-
46	SC	17/03/2017	CR51	4002	Printer Accessorie	0	T1	301.52			301.52	N	-
55	SR	19/03/2017		1200	Sales Receipt	0	T9	1,565.82			1,565.82	-	R
					Totals:			1,105.20	1,105.20	2,972.54	1,867.34		

Amount Outstanding	1,105.20
Amount Paid this period	1,565.82
Credit Limit £	12,500.00
Turnover YTD	2,537.07

Supplier Activity (detailed report)

Date:	23/08/2017	**Way to Work Ltd**	Page: 1
Time:	12:56:27	**Supplier Activity (Detailed)**	

Date From:	01/01/1980		Supplier From:	
Date To:	31/03/2017		Supplier To:	ZZZZZZZZ
Transaction From:	1		N/C From:	
Transaction To:	99,999,999		N/C To:	99999999
Inc b/fwd transaction:	No		Dept From:	0
Exc later payment:	No		Dept To:	999

** NOTE: All report values are shown in Base Currency, unless otherwise indicated **

A/C:	SP01	Name:	Paper Products UK			Contact:					Tel:			

No	Type	Date	Ref	N/C	Details	Dept	T/C	Value	O/S	Debit	Credit	V	B
5	PI	28/02/2017	0165	9998	Opening Balance	0	T9	445.23	0.00		445.23	-	-
47	PI	10/03/2017	0200	5000	Stationery	0	T1	586.80 *	586.80		586.80	N	-
56	PP	31/03/2017	CANCEL	1200	Purchase Payment	0	T9	445.23	0.00	445.23		-	R
66	PR	31/03/2017	CANCEL	1200	Cancelled Cheque	0	T9	445.23	445.23		445.23	-	R
					Totals:			1,032.03	1,032.03	445.23	1,477.26		

Amount Outstanding	1,032.03
Amount paid this period	0.00
Credit Limit £	8,500.00
Turnover YTD	934.23

A/C:	SP02	Name:	Wallace & Gromit Ltd.			Contact:					Tel:			

No	Type	Date	Ref	N/C	Details	Dept	T/C	Value	O/S	Debit	Credit	V	B
6	PI	11/02/2017	02183	9998	Opening Balance	0	T9	6,711.00 *	6,711.00		6,711.00	-	-
48	PI	11/03/2017	02241	5001	CD Roms	0	T1	414.00 *	414.00		414.00	N	-
					Totals:			7,125.00	7,125.00	0.00	7,125.00		

Amount Outstanding	7,125.00
Amount paid this period	0.00
Credit Limit £	12,000.00
Turnover YTD	7,056.00

A/C:	SP03	Name:	Whole Office Furniture			Contact:					Tel:			

No	Type	Date	Ref	N/C	Details	Dept	T/C	Value	O/S	Debit	Credit	V	B
7	PI	26/02/2017	1028	9998	Opening Balance	0	T9	1,875.21	0.00		1,875.21	-	-
49	PI	11/03/2017	1098	5002	Printer Accessories	0	T1	9,153.60 *	9,153.60		9,153.60	N	-
57	PP	31/03/2017	100077	1200	Purchase Payment	0	T9	1,875.21	0.00	1,875.21		-	R
					Totals:			9,153.60	9,153.60	1,875.21	11,028.81		

Amount Outstanding	9,153.60
Amount paid this period	1,875.21
Credit Limit £	4,000.00
Turnover YTD	9,503.21

A/C:	SP04	Name:	Stationery World			Contact:					Tel:			

No	Type	Date	Ref	N/C	Details	Dept	T/C	Value	O/S	Debit	Credit	V	B
8	PI	18/02/2017	0187	9998	Opening Balance	0	T9	9,504.32	0.00		9,504.32	-	-
50	PI	14/03/2017	0197	5000	Stationery	0	T1	4,280.40 *	4,280.40		4,280.40	N	-
51	PC	19/03/2017	RF287	5000	Stationery	0	T1	148.90 *	-148.90	148.90		N	-
58	PP	31/03/2017	100078	1200	Purchase Payment	0	T9	9,504.32	0.00	9,504.32		-	N
					Totals:			4,131.50	4,131.50	9,653.22	13,784.72		

Amount Outstanding	4,131.50
Amount paid this period	9,504.32
Credit Limit £	16,500.00
Turnover YTD	12,947.24

Period Trial Balance for the month of March

Date:	23/08/2017	**Way to Work Ltd**	Page:	1
Time:	12:57:00	**Period Trial Balance**		

To Period: Month 12, December 2017

N/C	Name	Debit	Credit
0040	Furniture and Fixtures	8,000.00	
0050	Motor Vehicles	14,000.00	
1100	Debtors Control Account	18,474.00	
1200	Bank Current Account		2,144.53
1210	Bank Deposit Account	1,500.00	
1230	Petty Cash	206.68	
2100	Creditors Control Account		21,442.13
2200	Sales Tax Control Account		2,519.33
2201	Purchase Tax Control Account	2,463.20	
3000	Capital		34,000.00
3260	Drawings	1,000.00	
4000	Stationery Sales		7,893.73
4001	CD Roms Sales		1,776.00
4002	Printer Accessory Sales		14,527.63
5000	Stationery Purchases	6,331.92	
5001	CD Rom Purchases	555.00	
5002	Printer Accessory Purchases	22,628.00	
6201	Advertising	327.00	
7005	Wages and Salaries	5,700.00	
7100	Rent	2,668.00	
7200	Electricity	84.10	
7803	General Expenses	242.00	
7901	Bank Charges	123.45	
	Totals:	84,303.35	84,303.35

Audit Trail for March

Date	23/08/2017				**Way to Work Ltd**						Page:	1
Time:	12:57:41				**Audit Trail (Detailed)**							

Date From:	01/03/2017	Customer From:	
Date To:	31/03/2017	Customer To:	ZZZZZZZZ
Transaction From:	1	Supplier From:	
Transaction To:	99,999,999	Supplier To:	ZZZZZZZZ

Exclude Deleted Tran: No

No	Type	A/C	N/C	Dept	Details	Date	Ref	Net	Tax	T/C	Pd	Paid	V	B	Bank Rec. Date
9	JD	0050				01/03/2017	O/Bal	14,000.00	0.00		Y	14,000.00	-		
		9	0050	0	Opening Balance			14,000.00	0.00	T9		14,000.00	-		
10	JC	9998				01/03/2017	O/Bal	14,000.00	0.00		Y	14,000.00	-		
		10	9998	0	Opening Balance			14,000.00	0.00	T9		14,000.00	-		
11	JD	0040				01/03/2017	O/Bal	8,000.00	0.00		Y	8,000.00	-		
		11	0040	0	Opening Balance			8,000.00	0.00	T9		8,000.00	-		
12	JC	9998				01/03/2017	O/Bal	8,000.00	0.00		Y	8,000.00	-		
		12	9998	0	Opening Balance			8,000.00	0.00	T9		8,000.00	-		
13	JD	1200				01/03/2017	O/Bal	6,210.81	0.00		Y	6,210.81	-		31/03/2017
		13	1200	0	Opening Balance			6,210.81	0.00	T9		6,210.81	-		
14	JC	9998				01/03/2017	O/Bal	6,210.81	0.00		Y	6,210.81	-		
		14	9998	0	Opening Balance			6,210.81	0.00	T9		6,210.81	-		
15	JD	1230				01/03/2017	O/Bal	100.00	0.00		Y	100.00	-		31/03/2017
		15	1230	0	Opening Balance			100.00	0.00	T9		100.00	-		
16	JC	9998				01/03/2017	O/Bal	100.00	0.00		Y	100.00	-		
		16	9998	0	Opening Balance			100.00	0.00	T9		100.00	-		
17	JC	3000				01/03/2017	O/Bal	34,000.00	0.00		Y	34,000.00	-		
		17	3000	0	Opening Balance			34,000.00	0.00	T9		34,000.00	-		
18	JD	9998				01/03/2017	O/Bal	34,000.00	0.00		Y	34,000.00	-		
		18	9998	0	Opening Balance			34,000.00	0.00	T9		34,000.00	-		
19	JD	3260				01/03/2017	O/Bal	1,000.00	0.00		Y	1,000.00	-		
		19	3260	0	Opening Balance			1,000.00	0.00	T9		1,000.00	-		
20	JC	9998				01/03/2017	O/Bal	1,000.00	0.00		Y	1,000.00			

Date:	23/08/2017					Way to Work Ltd						Page:	2
Time:	12:57:41					Audit Trail (Detailed)							

No	Type	A/C	N/C	Dept	Details	Date	Ref	Net	Tax	T/C	Pd	Paid	V	B	Bank Rec. Date
		20	9998	0	Opening Balance			1,000.00	0.00	T9		1,000.00	-		
21	JC	4000				01/03/2017	O/Bal	903.73	0.00		Y	903.73			
		21	4000	0	Opening Balance			903.73	0.00	T9		903.73	-		
22	JD	9998				01/03/2017	O/Bal	903.73	0.00		Y	903.73			
		22	9998	0	Opening Balance			903.73	0.00	T9		903.73	-		
23	JC	4001				01/03/2017	O/Bal	855.00	0.00		Y	855.00			
		23	4001	0	Opening Balance			855.00	0.00	T9		855.00	-		
24	JD	9998				01/03/2017	O/Bal	855.00	0.00		Y	855.00			
		24	9998	0	Opening Balance			855.00	0.00	T9		855.00	-		
25	JC	4002				01/03/2017	O/Bal	9,842.00	0.00		Y	9,842.00			
		25	4002	0	Opening Balance			9,842.00	0.00	T9		9,842.00	-		
26	JD	9998				01/03/2017	O/Bal	9,842.00	0.00		Y	9,842.00			
		26	9998	0	Opening Balance			9,842.00	0.00	T9		9,842.00	-		
27	JD	5000				01/03/2017	O/Bal	2,400.00	0.00		Y	2,400.00			
		27	5000	0	Opening Balance			2,400.00	0.00	T9		2,400.00	-		
28	JC	9998				01/03/2017	O/Bal	2,400.00	0.00		Y	2,400.00			
		28	9998	0	Opening Balance			2,400.00	0.00	T9		2,400.00	-		
29	JD	5001				01/03/2017	O/Bal	210.00	0.00		Y	210.00			
		29	5001	0	Opening Balance			210.00	0.00	T9		210.00	-		
30	JC	9998				01/03/2017	O/Bal	210.00	0.00		Y	210.00			
		30	9998	0	Opening Balance			210.00	0.00	T9		210.00	-		
31	JD	5002				01/03/2017	O/Bal	15,000.00	0.00		Y	15,000.00			
		31	5002	0	Opening Balance			15,000.00	0.00	T9		15,000.00	-		
32	JC	9998				01/03/2017	O/Bal	15,000.00	0.00		Y	15,000.00			
		32	9998	0	Opening Balance			15,000.00	0.00	T9		15,000.00	-		
33	JD	7005				01/03/2017	O/Bal	5,600.00	0.00		Y	5,600.00			
		33	7005	0	Opening Balance			5,600.00	0.00	T9		5,600.00	-		
34	JC	9998				01/03/2017	O/Bal	5,600.00	0.00		Y	5,600.00			
		34	9998	0	Opening Balance			5,600.00	0.00	T9		5,600.00	-		

Date:	23/08/2017					Way to Work Ltd						Page:	3
Time:	12:57:41					Audit Trail (Detailed)							

No	Type	A/C	N/C	Dept	Details	Date	Ref	Net	Tax	T/C	Pd	Paid	V	B	Bank Rec. Date
35	JD	7803				01/03/2017	O/Bal	342.00	0.00		Y	342.00	-		
		35	7803	0	Opening Balance			342.00	0.00	T9		342.00	-		
36	JC	9998				01/03/2017	O/Bal	342.00	0.00		Y	342.00	-		
		36	9998	0	Opening Balance			342.00	0.00	T9		342.00	-		
37	JD	7100				01/03/2017	O/Bal	2,100.00	0.00		Y	2,100.00	-		
		37	7100	0	Opening Balance			2,100.00	0.00	T9		2,100.00	-		
38	JC	9998				01/03/2017	O/Bal	2,100.00	0.00		Y	2,100.00	-		
		38	9998	0	Opening Balance			2,100.00	0.00	T9		2,100.00	-		
39	JC	1200				01/03/2017	TRANS01	1,500.00	0.00		Y	1,500.00	R	31/03/2017
		39	1200	0	Bank Transfer			1,500.00	0.00	T9		1,500.00	-		
40	JD	1210				01/03/2017	TRANS01	1,500.00	0.00		Y	1,500.00	N	
		40	1210	0	Bank Transfer			1,500.00	0.00	T9		1,500.00	-		
41	SI	JP02				03/03/2017	INV041	780.00	156.00		N	0.00	-		
		41	4000	0	Stationery			780.00	156.00	T1		0.00	N		
42	SI	JP04				03/03/2017	INV042	921.00	184.20		N	0.00	-		
		42	4001	0	CD Roms			921.00	184.20	T1		0.00	N		
43	SI	JP01				05/03/2017	INV043	4,376.00	875.20		N	0.00	-		
		43	4002	0	Printer Accessory			4,376.00	875.20	T1		0.00	N		
44	SI	JP03				07/03/2017	INV044	458.00	91.60		N	0.00	-		
		44	4002	0	Printer Accessory			458.00	91.60	T1		0.00	N		
45	SI	JP01				07/03/2017	INV045	6,210.00	1,242.00		N	0.00	-		
		45	4000	0	Stationery			6,210.00	1,242.00	T1		0.00	N		
46	SC	JP04				17/03/2017	CR51	251.27	50.25		Y	301.52	-		
		46	4002	0	Printer Accessorie			251.27	50.25	T1		301.52	N		
					301.52 to SI 4	17/03/2017	INV34					301.52			
47	PI	SP01				10/03/2017	0200	489.00	97.80		N	0.00	-		
		47	5000	0	Stationery			489.00	97.80	T1		0.00	N		
48	PI	SP02				11/03/2017	02241	345.00	69.00		N	0.00	-		
		48	5001	0	CD Roms			345.00	69.00	T1		0.00	N		

KAPLAN PUBLISHING

Date:	23/08/2017						**Way to Work Ltd**						Page:	4
Time:	12:57:41						**Audit Trail (Detailed)**							

No	Type	A/C	N/C	Dept	Details	Date	Ref	Net	Tax	T/C	Pd	Paid	V	B	Bank Rec. Date
49	PI	SP03				11/03/2017	1098	7,628.00	1,525.60		N	0.00	-		
		49	5002	0	Printer Accessories			7,628.00	1,525.60	T1		0.00	N		
50	PI	SP04				14/03/2017	0197	3,567.00	713.40		N	0.00	-		
		50	5000	0	Stationery			3,567.00	713.40	T1		0.00	N		
51	PC	SP04				19/03/2017	RF287	124.08	24.82		N	0.00	-		
		51	5000	0	Stationery			124.08	24.82	T1		0.00	N		
52	BR	1200				28/03/2017	ST4	102.90	20.58		Y	123.48		R	31/03/2017
		52	4002	0	Printer Accessories			102.90	20.58	T1		123.48	N		
53	SR	JP01				15/03/2017		1,172.34	0.00		Y	1,172.34		R	31/03/2017
		53	1200	0	Sales Receipt			1,172.34	0.00	T9		1,172.34	-		
					1172.34 to SI 1	15/03/2017	INV021					1,172.34			
54	SR	JP02				17/03/2017		2,954.00	0.00		Y	2,954.00		R	31/03/2017
		54	1200	0	Sales Receipt			2,954.00	0.00	T9		2,954.00	-		
					2954.00 to SI 2	17/03/2017	INV045					2,954.00			
55	SR	JP04				19/03/2017		1,565.82	0.00		Y	1,565.82		R	31/03/2017
		55	1200	0	Sales Receipt			1,565.82	0.00	T9		1,565.82	-		
					1565.82 to SI 4	19/03/2017	INV34					1,565.82			
56	PP	SP01				31/03/2017	CANCEL	445.23	0.00		Y	445.23		R	31/03/2017
		56	1200	0	Purchase Payment			445.23	0.00	T9		445.23	-		
					445.23 to PI 5	31/03/2017	0165					445.23			
57	PP	SP03				31/03/2017	100077	1,875.21	0.00		Y	1,875.21		R	31/03/2017
		57	1200	0	Purchase Payment			1,875.21	0.00	T9		1,875.21	-		
					1875.21 to PI 7	31/03/2017	1028					1,875.21			
58	PP	SP04				31/03/2017	100078	9,504.32	0.00		Y	9,504.32		N	
		58	1200	0	Purchase Payment			9,504.32	0.00	T9		9,504.32	-		
					9504.32 to PI 8	31/03/2017	0187					9,504.32			
59	BP	1200				31/03/2017	DD/STO	568.00	0.00		Y	568.00		R	31/03/2017
		59	7100	0	ICPW Bank			568.00	0.00	T9		568.00	-		
60	CP	1230				19/03/2017	056	84.10	16.82		Y	100.92	-		
		60	7200	0	Electricity			84.10	16.82	T1		100.92	N		

Date:	23/08/2017						**Way to Work Ltd**						Page:	5
Time:	12:57:41						**Audit Trail (Detailed)**							

No	Type	A/C	N/C	Dept	Details	Date	Ref	Net	Tax	T/C	Pd	Paid	V	B	Bank Rec. Date
61	CP	1230				20/03/2017	057	327.00	65.40		Y	392.40	-		
		61	6201	0	Advertising			327.00	65.40	T1		392.40	N		
62	JD	7005				25/03/2017	JNL001	100.00	0.00		Y	100.00	-		
		62	7005	0	Being the transfer of			100.00	0.00	T9		100.00	-		
63	JC	7803				25/03/2017	JNL001	100.00	0.00		Y	100.00	-		
		63	7803	0	Being the transfer of			100.00	0.00	T9		100.00	-		
64	JC	1200				15/03/2017	TRANS02	600.00	0.00		Y	600.00		R	31/03/2017
		64	1200	0	Bank Transfer			600.00	0.00	T9		600.00	-		
65	JD	1230				15/03/2017	TRANS02	600.00	0.00		Y	600.00	-		
		65	1230	0	Bank Transfer			600.00	0.00	T9		600.00	-		
66	PR	SP01				31/03/2017	CANCEL	445.23	0.00		N	0.00		R	31/03/2017
		66	1200	0	Cancelled Cheque			445.23	0.00	T9		0.00	-		
67	BP	1200				31/03/2017		123.45	0.00		Y	123.45		R	31/03/2017
		67	7901	0	Charges incurred			123.45	0.00	T2		123.45	N		

Nominal Ledger Activity for Bank/Petty Cash

| Date: | 23/08/2017 | | | | | **Way to Work Ltd** | | | | Page: | 1 |
| Time: | 12:58:36 | | | | | **Nominal Activity** | | | | | |

| Date From: | 01/01/1980 | N/C From: | |
| Date To: | 31/03/2017 | N/C To: | 99999999 |

| Transaction From: | 1 |
| Transaction To: | 99,999,999 |

| N/C: | 1200 | | Name: | Bank Current Account | | | | | Account Balance: | | 2,144.53 CR |

No	Type	Date	Account	Ref	Details	Dept	T/C	Value	Debit	Credit	V	B
13	JD	01/03/2017	1200	O/Bal	Opening Balance	0	T9	6,210.81	6,210.81		-	-
39	JC	01/03/2017	1200	TRANS01	Bank Transfer	0	T9	1,500.00		1,500.00	-	R
52	BR	28/03/2017	1200	ST4	Printer Accessories	0	T1	123.48	123.48		N	R
53	SR	15/03/2017	JP01		Sales Receipt	0	T9	1,172.34	1,172.34		-	R
54	SR	17/03/2017	JP02		Sales Receipt	0	T9	2,954.00	2,954.00		-	R
55	SR	19/03/2017	JP04		Sales Receipt	0	T9	1,565.82	1,565.82		-	R
56	PP	31/03/2017	SP01	CANCEL	Purchase Payment	0	T9	445.23		445.23	-	R
57	PP	31/03/2017	SP03	100077	Purchase Payment	0	T9	1,875.21		1,875.21	-	R
58	PP	31/03/2017	SP04	100078	Purchase Payment	0	T9	9,504.32		9,504.32	-	N
59	BP	31/03/2017	1200	DD/STO	ICPW Bank	0	T9	568.00		568.00	-	R
64	JC	15/03/2017	1200	TRANS02	Bank Transfer	0	T9	600.00		600.00	-	R
66	PR	31/03/2017	SP01	CANCEL	Cancelled Cheque	0	T9	445.23	445.23		-	R
67	BP	31/03/2017	1200		Charges incurred	0	T2	123.45		123.45	N	R
							Totals:		12,471.68	14,616.21		
							History Balance:			2,144.53		

| N/C: | 1230 | | Name: | Petty Cash | | | | | Account Balance: | | 206.68 DR |

No	Type	Date	Account	Ref	Details	Dept	T/C	Value	Debit	Credit	V	B
15	JD	01/03/2017	1230	O/Bal	Opening Balance	0	T9	100.00	100.00		-	-
60	CP	19/03/2017	1230	056	Electricity	0	T1	100.92		100.92	N	-
61	CP	20/03/2017	1230	057	Advertising	0	T1	392.40		392.40	N	-
65	JD	15/03/2017	1230	TRANS02	Bank Transfer	0	T9	600.00	600.00		-	-
							Totals:		700.00	493.32		
							History Balance:		206.68			

Sales Day Book

| Date: | 23/08/2017 | | | | | **Way to Work Ltd** | | | | Page: | 1 |
| Time: | 12:59:14 | | | | | **Day Books: Customer Invoices (Detailed)** | | | | | |

| Date From: | 01/01/1980 | Customer From: | |
| Date To: | 31/12/2019 | Customer To: | ZZZZZZZZ |

| Transaction From: | 1 | N/C From: | |
| Transaction To: | 99,999,999 | N/C To: | 99999999 |

| Dept From: | 0 |
| Dept To: | 999 |

Tran No.	Type	Date	A/C Ref	N/C	Inv Ref	Dept.	Details	Net Amount	Tax Amount	T/C	Gross Amount	V	B
1	SI	14/02/2017	JP01	9998	INV021	0	Opening Balance	1,172.34	0.00	T9	1,172.34	-	-
2	SI	22/02/2017	JP02	9998	INV045	0	Opening Balance	2,954.00	0.00	T9	2,954.00	-	-
3	SI	18/02/2017	JP03	9998	INV033	0	Opening Balance	3,180.00	0.00	T9	3,180.00	-	-
4	SI	22/02/2017	JP04	9998	INV34	0	Opening Balance	1,867.34	0.00	T9	1,867.34	-	-
41	SI	03/03/2017	JP02	4000	INV041	0	Stationery	780.00	156.00	T1	936.00	N	-
42	SI	03/03/2017	JP04	4001	INV042	0	CD Roms	921.00	184.20	T1	1,105.20	N	-
43	SI	05/03/2017	JP01	4002	INV043	0	Printer Accessory	4,376.00	875.20	T1	5,251.20	N	-
44	SI	07/03/2017	JP03	4002	INV044	0	Printer Accessory	458.00	91.60	T1	549.60	N	-
45	SI	07/03/2017	JP01	4000	INV045	0	Stationery	6,210.00	1,242.00	T1	7,452.00	N	-
							Totals:	21,918.68	2,549.00		24,467.68		

Purchases Day Book

| Date: | 23/08/2017 | | | | | | **Way to Work Ltd** | | | | Page: | 1 |

Day Books: Supplier Invoices (Detailed)

Time: 12:59:39

| Date From: | 01/01/1980 | | Supplier From: | |
| Date To: | 31/12/2019 | | Supplier To: | ZZZZZZZZ |

| Transaction From: | 1 | | N/C From: | |
| Transaction To: | 99,999,999 | | N/C To: | 99999999 |

| Dept From: | 0 |
| Dept To: | 999 |

Tran No.	Type	Date	A/C Ref	N/C	Inv Ref	Dept	Details	Net Amount	Tax Amount	T/C	Gross Amount	V	B
5	PI	28/02/2017	SP01	9998	0165	0	Opening Balance	445.23	0.00	T9	445.23	-	-
6	PI	11/02/2017	SP02	9998	02183	0	Opening Balance	6,711.00	0.00	T9	6,711.00	-	-
7	PI	26/02/2017	SP03	9998	1028	0	Opening Balance	1,875.21	0.00	T9	1,875.21	-	-
8	PI	18/02/2017	SP04	9998	0187	0	Opening Balance	9,504.32	0.00	T9	9,504.32	-	-
47	PI	10/03/2017	SP01	5000	0200	0	Stationery	489.00	97.80	T1	586.80	N	-
48	PI	11/03/2017	SP02	5001	02241	0	CD Roms	345.00	69.00	T1	414.00	N	-
49	PI	11/03/2017	SP03	5002	1098	0	Printer Accessories	7,628.00	1,525.60	T1	9,153.60	N	-
50	PI	14/03/2017	SP04	5000	0197	0	Stationery	3,567.00	713.40	T1	4,280.40	N	-
							Totals	30,564.76	2,405.80		32,970.56		

Aged Creditors

| Date: | 23/08/2017 | | **Way to Work Ltd** | | Page: | 1 |

Aged Creditors Analysis (Detailed)

Time: 13:00:02

| Date From: | 01/01/1980 | | Supplier From: | |
| Date To: | 31/03/2017 | | Supplier To: | ZZZZZZZZ |

Include future transactions: No
Exclude later payments: No

** NOTE: All report values are shown in Base Currency, unless otherwise indicated **

A/C: SP01   Name: Paper Products UK   Contact: Tel:

No.	Type	Date	Ref	Details	Balance	Future	Current	Period 1	Period 2	Period 3	Older
47	PI	10/03/2017	0200	Stationery	586.80	0.00	586.80	0.00	0.00	0.00	0.00
66	PR	31/03/2017	CANCEL	Cancelled Cheque	445.23	0.00	445.23	0.00	0.00	0.00	0.00
				Totals:	1,032.03	0.00	1,032.03	0.00	0.00	0.00	0.00

Turnover: 934.23
Credit Limit £ 8,500.00

A/C: SP02   Name: Wallace & Gromit Ltd   Contact: Tel:

No.	Type	Date	Ref	Details	Balance	Future	Current	Period 1	Period 2	Period 3	Older
6	PI	11/02/2017	02183	Opening Balance	6,711.00	0.00	0.00	6,711.00	0.00	0.00	0.00
48	PI	11/03/2017	02241	CD Roms	414.00	0.00	414.00	0.00	0.00	0.00	0.00
				Totals:	7,125.00	0.00	414.00	6,711.00	0.00	0.00	0.00

Turnover: 7,056.00
Credit Limit £ 12,000.00

A/C: SP03   Name: Whole Office Furniture   Contact: Tel:

No.	Type	Date	Ref	Details	Balance	Future	Current	Period 1	Period 2	Period 3	Older
49	PI	11/03/2017	1098	Printer Accessories	9,153.60	0.00	9,153.60	0.00	0.00	0.00	0.00
				Totals:	9,153.60	0.00	9,153.60	0.00	0.00	0.00	0.00

Turnover: 9,503.21
Credit Limit £ 4,000.00

A/C: SP04   Name: Stationery World   Contact: Tel:

No.	Type	Date	Ref	Details	Balance	Future	Current	Period 1	Period 2	Period 3	Older
50	PI	14/03/2017	0197	Stationery	4,280.40	0.00	4,280.40	0.00	0.00	0.00	0.00
51	PC	19/03/2017	RF287	Stationery	-148.90	0.00	-148.90	0.00	0.00	0.00	0.00
				Totals:	4,131.50	0.00	4,131.50	0.00	0.00	0.00	0.00

Turnover: 12,947.24
Credit Limit £ 16,500.00

| | | | | **Grand Totals:** | 21,442.13 | 0.00 | 14,731.13 | 6,711.00 | 0.00 | 0.00 | 0.00 |

Aged Debtors

Way to Work Ltd

Aged Debtors Analysis (Detailed)

Page: 1

Date From:	01/01/1980		Customer From:	
Date To:	31/03/2017		Customer To:	ZZZZZZZZ
Include future transactions:	No			
Exclude later payments:	No			

** NOTE: All report values are shown in Base Currency, unless otherwise indicated **

| A/C: | JP01 | Name: | Morgan, Smith & Winston | | Contact: | | | Tel: | | |

No	Type	Date	Ref	Details	Balance	Future	Current	Period 1	Period 2	Period 3	Older
43	SI	05/03/2017	INV043	Printer Accessory	5,251.20	0.00	5,251.20	0.00	0.00	0.00	0.00
45	SI	07/03/2017	INV045	Stationery	7,452.00	0.00	7,452.00	0.00	0.00	0.00	0.00
				Totals:	12,703.20	0.00	12,703.20	0.00	0.00	0.00	0.00

Turnover: 11,758.34
Credit Limit £   7,000.00

| A/C: | JP02 | Name: | Cyril West | | Contact: | | | Tel: | | |

No	Type	Date	Ref	Details	Balance	Future	Current	Period 1	Period 2	Period 3	Older
41	SI	03/03/2017	INV041	Stationery	936.00	0.00	936.00	0.00	0.00	0.00	0.00
				Totals:	936.00	0.00	936.00	0.00	0.00	0.00	0.00

Turnover: 3,734.00
Credit Limit £   8,500.00

| A/C: | JP03 | Name: | Wallace & Gromit Ltd | | Contact: | | | Tel: | | |

No	Type	Date	Ref	Details	Balance	Future	Current	Period 1	Period 2	Period 3	Older
3	SI	18/02/2017	INV033	Opening Balance	3,180.00	0.00	0.00	3,180.00	0.00	0.00	0.00
44	SI	07/03/2017	INV044	Printer Accessory	549.60	0.00	549.60	0.00	0.00	0.00	0.00
				Totals:	3,729.60	0.00	549.60	3,180.00	0.00	0.00	0.00

Turnover: 3,638.00
Credit Limit £   17,000.00

| A/C: | JP04 | Name: | Star Paper | | Contact: | | | Tel: | | |

No	Type	Date	Ref	Details	Balance	Future	Current	Period 1	Period 2	Period 3	Older
42	SI	03/03/2017	INV042	CD Roms	1,105.20	0.00	1,105.20	0.00	0.00	0.00	0.00
				Totals:	1,105.20	0.00	1,105.20	0.00	0.00	0.00	0.00

Turnover: 2,537.07
Credit Limit £   12,500.00

| | | | | Grand Totals: | 18,474.00 | 0.00 | 15,294.00 | 3,180.00 | 0.00 | 0.00 | 0.00 |

Statement for Cyril West

Way to Work Ltd			
55 Upper Street			
London			
N1 9PE			

JP02

Cyril West	
Grays West	
Grays Inn Road	31/03/2017
London	
WC1 1LT	I

NOTE: All values are shown in Pound Sterling

22/02/17	INV045	Goods/Services	2,954.00	
03/03/17	INV041	Goods/Services	936.00 *	
17/03/17		Payment		2,954.00

Way to Work Ltd			
55 Upper Street			
London			
N1 9PE			

JP02

Cyril West	
Grays West	
Grays Inn Road	31/03/2017
London	
WC1 1LT	I

NOTE: All values are shown in **Pound Sterling**

22/02/17	Goods/Services	2,954.00	
03/03/17	Goods/Services	936.00	
17/03/17	Payment		2,954.00

£ 936.00 £ 0.00 £ 0.00 £ 0.00 £ 0.00

£ 936.00

£ 936.00

Bank Reconciliation (Reconciled Transactions)

Date: 23/08/2017
Time: 13:01:35

Way to Work Ltd

Bank Reconciled Transactions

Page: 1

Bank Reconciled On: 31/03/2017

No	Type	Date	A/C	N/C	Dept	Ref	Details	Net	Tax	T/C
13	JD	01/03/2017	1200	1200	0	O/Bal	Opening Balance	6,210.81	0.00	T9
39	JC	01/03/2017	1200	1200	0	TRANS01	Bank Transfer	1,500.00	0.00	T9
52	BR	28/03/2017	1200	4002	0	ST4	Printer Accessories	102.90	20.58	T1
53	SR	15/03/2017	JP01	1200	0		Sales Receipt	1,172.34	0.00	T9
54	SR	17/03/2017	JP02	1200	0		Sales Receipt	2,954.00	0.00	T9
55	SR	19/03/2017	JP04	1200	0		Sales Receipt	1,565.82	0.00	T9
56	PP	31/03/2017	SP01	1200	0	CANCEL	Purchase Payment	445.23	0.00	T9
57	PP	31/03/2017	SP03	1200	0	100077	Purchase Payment	1,875.21	0.00	T9
59	BP	31/03/2017	1200	7100	0	DD/STO	ICPW Bank	568.00	0.00	T9
64	JC	15/03/2017	1200	1200	0	TRANS02	Bank Transfer	600.00	0.00	T9
66	PR	31/03/2017	SP01	1200	0	CANCEL	Cancelled Cheque	445.23	0.00	T9
67	BP	31/03/2017	1200	7901	0		Charges incurred	123.45	0.00	T2